Son of a Preacher Man
Matthew Gregorowski

First published by Busybird Publishing 2024
Copyright © 2024 TMT Foundation Pty Limited

ISBN:
Print (paperback): 978-1-7636453-0-1
Ebook: 978-1-7636453-1-8

This work is copyright. Apart from any use permitted under the *Copyright Act 1968*, no part of this publication may be reproduced, stored in a retrieval system or transmitted in any form or by any means, electronic, mechanical, photocopying, recording or otherwise, without the prior written permission of TMT Foundation Pty Limited.

The information in this book is based on the author's experiences and opinions. The author and publisher disclaim responsibility for any adverse consequences, which may result from use of the information contained herein. Permission to use any external content has been sought by the author. Any breaches will be rectified in further editions of the book.

Cover Image: Rob Perry Design & Art Direction

Cover design: Rob Perry Design & Art Direction

Layout and typesetting: Busybird Publishing

Busybird Publishing
2/118 Para Road
Montmorency, Victoria
Australia 3094
www.busybird.com.au

For
Mum and Dad

Introduction

Have you ever felt that there is something missing in your life but you can't quite put your finger on it? And no matter how much you distract yourself with the business of life, when you slow down enough to notice, it's always there? It happens to most of us because we are not living our true purpose.

Many of us just ignore it or continue to distract ourselves with the next shiny new thing. Or we look for the answers in our careers or relationships. I tried all of those things but the nagging only grew louder, like an itch you just can't reach.

Growing up in an Anglican rectory during South Africa's apartheid era, I was constantly confronted by rules that I neither understood nor appreciated. They instilled in me a yearning to find my own freedoms. But they also ingrained in me a deep respect for my father, who from an early age dedicated his life to the service of others.

It was only in charting my own course, beyond the confines of home and country, that I would come to realise that the path to finding my answers lay in first understanding my father. I needed to experience what he felt in his heart, and to know God as he does.

What started as a tool for managing anxiety became an ingrained meditation practice that has laid the answers before me, clear as day. But it has also cracked open the boundaries of my perception and thrust me into a brave new world. It was only by looking within that I began living a life in which I will never go without.

We are, all of us, called on to find and live out our true purpose. And when we do, all that we perceive as life's stresses and struggles gradually disappear and we start living in harmony with one another and the world around us. This is how we create a world at peace with itself. It is not a utopian dream, it is right here within our grasp.

Buddha said 'Your purpose in life is to find your purpose and give your whole heart and soul to it … those who have failed to work toward the truth have missed the purpose of living.'

CONTENTS

Introduction   i

Part I
GENESIS

1	Guiding hands	3
2	Wonderland	11
3	Like father …	21
4	Forging a new path	33
5	Death becomes you	41
6	Touched by an angel	51
7	London calling	69
8	Human traffic	81
9	No spare room for denial	87

Part II
THE GOSPEL

10	The model, the military man and the monk	97
11	Charl and his angels	103
12	Victoria's privilege	137
13	Jude's calling	171

PART III
REVELATIONS

14	… Like son: confronting self	197
15	The power of one	205
16	The science of flow	221
17	Hey Megan, turn it down	235
18	The ego trap	253
19	Heaven on earth	261

Acknowledgements   269
Endnotes   271

Part I

GENESIS

1
Guiding hands

Of all my father's features, it is his hands that I know most intricately. Walking into his study at night as a child, they were the first thing I noticed. His right hand wielding a black Parker fountain pen and his left hand resting on the familiar green ink blotter.

Perhaps this was because his hands symbolised so much about him. His authority, raised to the heavens in praise before the altar. His stewardship, administering the Holy Eucharist to his kneeling parishioners. His devotion, clasped before him in earnest prayer. And his empathy, hands laid on those in their time of need: for me that came at the age of five, one of my first memories of Dad. I had repetitive nightmares of a world drifting further and further away as I screamed into a vacuum, engulfed by darkness. It's when the bedwetting started.

They'd honed it into a neat double act, Mum whipping on clean sheets and Dad laying his hands on me, always the stomach and forehead. He prayed aloud, calling on God to relieve me of my anguish, to bring me peace.

Paralysed with the fear that I'd fall back to sleep, I'd gradually feel an intense serenity. Under his hands I knew that nothing could take me away from safety and that I was exactly where I needed to be. These were my first real encounters with God.

Dad was posted in Bredasdorp – a farming town near Africa's southern-most point, Cape Agulhas – as the rector at All Saints Anglican Church. It was there that I enjoyed a relatively carefree childhood, running barefoot through its sleepy streets with my friends and neighbours, like it was our fiefdom. For the most part they were Afrikaner kids from the all-white NG Kerk, the Dutch Reformed Church of South Africa, a staunchly traditional institution that took the Bible at its literal core and considered the servitude of black people under apartheid to be their God-given right.

Our days at Bredasdorp Laerskool (Primary) started with morning assembly, hands on hearts singing Die Stem – the Afrikaner national anthem – under the judicious gaze of our principal. Hair slicked back, clipped moustache and rigid with attention, he might well have been mistaken for the Führer while on the back wall an orange, white and blue Republic of South Africa flag towered like a badge of honour.

In my naïve youth I was oblivious to the machinations of social order. We fought over the attention of girls, not the conflicting beliefs of our parents and side by side we played rugby against visiting teams whose religious and political affiliations were far more aligned with my own. We were united in our innocence and voyages of discovery, from opposite sides of an invisible line.

Mum and Dad on the other hand knew it well and navigated it deftly, happy to set aside their opinions in the interests of social cohesion. But it wasn't easy. At first, they'd been welcomed with open arms, invited to any number of community lunches and boxed wine braais, or barbecues. But as soon as the young couple's true colours came out, the offers dried up like turpentine on tarmac.

As with all towns during apartheid, Bredasdorp was racially segregated. The leafy town centre and its salubrious surrounds were the preserve of the well-to-do whites, while everyone else was sequestered to the outskirts called the 'onderdorp'. The driveways off the gravel roads were mostly empty, while children played in dusty, hen-pecked yards.

It's where the town's mostly mixed-race communities lived and thrived. Known colloquially and just as affectionately as Cape Coloureds, they descended largely from Dutch settlers who found solace in the arms of native Xhosa and Khoisan people and of slaves brought to South Africa by Arab traders. Famous for their penchant for cooking, these were vibrant communities that more than made up for their lack of means through an abundance of spirit. Their language was as colourful as they were, in many instances aided by missing the top four front teeth. Today it's fashionably called the 'passion gap', but many believe it stemmed from their captive forebears who removed teeth as a way to take back control from their captors, the value of slaves often determined by the quality of their teeth.

All Saints Church, with its brushed sandstone walls and thatched roof, stood resplendent at the top of Long Street. Dad's task there was to engender interracial services – much to the chagrin of the State – and to introduce the Anglican renewal movement, an evangelical form of worship based on empowerment of the Holy Spirit. Despite his best efforts the white farmers preferred services in English, while coloured parishioners from the onderdorp were forced to sweat up the long hill in their Sunday best to listen to services held in their native Afrikaans. And when Dad pushed the unification agenda too hard, many of his friends absconded to the all-white Methodist church at the other end of town.

It broke his heart, so instead he sought permission from then archbishop, Bill Burnet, for the Diocese to jointly fund a plot of land near the onderdorp and build a new church for 600 parishioners. It would save them the indignity of worshipping in a white man's church; the white man had given them one of their own. Then he took a blowtorch to its spiritual tinder box and lifted the roof right off the place. Vibrant songs of praise permeated Sunday morning skies as parishioners and visitors alike flocked to the shiny new redbrick house of God.

There was mid-week house church in our sitting room too, a handful of the most faithful praying and singing to the hypnotic rhythms of Dad's acoustic guitar. A 'gift of the spirit', he still calls it. He'd barely known a few chords and certainly can't remember any now. But in the pale candlelight of our Bredasdorp sitting room, Dad's black wavy locks might well have been mistaken for Dylan.

Hands aloft they'd pray in unison, speaking in tongues, lost to this world in their connection with God. Mum was always front and centre and she talks about that time with great fondness. It was a gift one had to ask for, to be empowered by the Holy Spirit as a vessel for prayer. To communicate from within and ask for healing, for other people or for the nation, or whatever it was that would be God's will.

Her thoughts were always lucid, but the language was nonsensical, tapping into the energy drawn both from within and from one another, channelling as a collective. To a small child watching from the hallway of our Bredasdorp home, it was as electric as it was mystifying. It is only now so much later in life that I can comprehend those moments of free consciousness as I encounter my own.

oOo

Dad had been sent to Bredasdorp after the area he'd served in – District Six – was torn down by the apartheid government. I was just 18 months old when our orange VW Beatle left the once-vibrant community behind in the rear-view mirror, Richard in the back seat and me in the arms of our nanny, Cathy Whiteman. She was an unmarried and devoted fifty-plus coloured parishioner who'd spent her life taking care of sick parents and raising her two siblings. Born on the wrong side of apartheid, she'd been denied any formal education and when her own parents passed away, Cathy became part of the family.

Her bashful smile hid behind straight dark hair and soulful eyes; in every respect she epitomised the model human being, her devotion to God was unbounded. Each day started and finished with readings from the Holy Bible, always beside her on the bedside table. She practised a deep-rooted, authentic gratefulness to the Lord above for the clothes on her back, roof over her head and a plate of food to keep her nourished. And for her new-found sense of purpose in helping to raise her two boys.

Mum, meanwhile, had made no secret of wanting daughters so Cathy being one of the family was always part of the plan. Not long after we arrived in Bredasdorp, prayers were offered in earnest and promptly answered: Sarah Elizabeth arrived eighteen months later followed by Claire Theresa, rounding off the perfect brood. With Mum looking after the girls, it was those early years under Cathy's dutiful care that undoubtedly helped shape my moral compass. There was an innocence and purity about her to which only a young child could relate and throughout my life I have drawn from her example.

The fact that she was living with us illegally was never raised and if she was ever worried, she never let on. To a young child it made the concept of apartheid quite bewildering. Why would anyone not want me spending time with Cathy? Why was it wrong for her to live in our house, or come out with us for supper? It was a strange set of rules I simply couldn't fathom.

Fish Hoek Beach along the Cape's southern coast was a haven where we spent many sun-soaked weekends, all buckets, spades and floppy hats. It's where Mum had grown up and her parents weren't the venturing kind. To get there from Kalk Bay parking lot we had to walk through a tunnel under the main road, at the end of which were two archways. We'd veer right under the 'Whites Only' plaque without giving it a second thought, but every so often I'd stop to look over my shoulder. Coloured families sat crammed between kelp-covered rock pools, gannets screeching overhead for discarded scraps of take-away fish and chips. Through the haze of churning seaweed, bird shit and salt and vinegar, children cavorted while parents shared funny stories, oblivious to the little white boy, gawking.

While bemused, at first I just accepted it as the way things were. But as the colour of my perceptions deepened it was hard to ignore the growing unease I felt. As a teenager my friends and I would often take the train to Muizenberg, our favourite surf beach. Flopping about our first-class seats I'd force myself to stare at the waves crashing against the seawall barricade, to avoid eye contact with the coloured and black kids squeezed against the adjoining third class carriage window.

I'd wonder what was going through their minds, how it must feel to be so marginalised in this place we all called home. When I was on my own, I'd often ride 'third class' just so I didn't have to wear the guilt. Despite the questioning eyes I never sensed any danger. These were just people going about their everyday lives. And what irked me more than anything was how out of place I was made to feel in my own country. Perhaps, in that way alone, I could share some affinity with my countrymen.

It was one of many ways that throughout my childhood I felt like a fish out of water. I have long since lost contact with my Bredasdorp school friends; I still remember them fondly not because of anything they represented but because they were good people. Yet I have no idea what could have gone through their hearts and minds the day Nelson Mandela walked free from Robben Island or when the president and leader of the National Party, FW de Klerk, conceded government to the African National Congress.

Perhaps it's just better that way.

2
Wonderland

District Six was a wondrously eclectic community that thousands of coloured people called home. It was a melting pot of languages, religions and ethnic backgrounds which became known for harmonic diversity, flying at the very heart of the apartheid government's segregation agenda.

Set at the foothills of Table Mountain and close to the city centre, it was a prime location much more suited to housing a white police force and former President Hendrik Verwoerd declared the area a whites-only zone under the Group Areas Act of 1950. This was despite less than 1% of its people being white, our family among them. It meant that from 1968 until the last bulldozers retreated in 1982, more than 60 000 people would be forcibly relocated to a bleak, sandy township complex some 25 kilometres away: the Cape Flats.

It was a devastating time not only for the good people of District Six, but also for the country. To this day, their forced removal at the hands of South Africa's vicious and oppressive regime is one of the greatest blights in its history.

Despite their physical separation, the emotional umbilical cord was still firmly intact. They renamed their new barren and windswept home Hanover Park, after Hanover Street that ran like an aorta through the middle of District Six where they returned on Sundays, rising before dawn to make the long journey back by bus and train, faithful to their roots and their priest, their true home. In their third-class carriages they rattled around like the third-class citizens they were made to feel, but at the end of the line they walked tall down Hope Street to the one place where they were loved unconditionally.

Dad had been tasked with uniting the parishes of downtown St Philips and also of St Marks further up the hill, remembered for its fine sandstone walls and shiny red roof. But what he quickly realised was that having lost nearly everything else, the last thing these good people needed was to lose the churches, standing as the last beacons of hope among District Six's rag-tag of beaten up townhouses and poverty-scuffed alleys. They just needed him to befriend them, to accept them and to love them and he did it with fervour. Standing in the pulpit he would say to his congregations, 'You know, I really love you' and mean it. It was a watershed moment in his ministry, finally understanding God's love for every one of us.

But as noble as it was to run two parishes, two sets of services, Church councils, Sunday schools, mothers' unions, home visits and baptisms all while trying to support Mum to raise two young boys, it took its toll. The work of saving souls doesn't start at nine and finish at five and by the time he'd get home, Richard and I were long bathed, fed and fast asleep.

Mum bore numerous other responsibilities too and from early on she knew her life would be one of self-sacrifice. To marry a priest is to marry the church and her devotion was no less that Dad's. As figureheads in the community they were always leading a life of example. It was a conscious decision and one she made willingly out of her love for God as well for Dad.

She taught Sunday School, ran the Anglican Women's Fellowship, managed the church grounds, organised charitable donations, arranged the church flowers, visited the lonely and fed the stream of homeless people who knocked on our door. But most magnanimously of all, she accompanied Dad to every function, with two lots of doting congregants to care for.

As gregarious as my father was, my mother was an introvert who found little solace in those early years. What pumped up his tyres, deflated hers and loving a man beholden to God above all else, including her, carried with it an emotional millstone. But it would only be years later that I came to realise the true nature of her sacrifice.

Not quite a teenager and living then in the Cape Town suburb of Lansdowne, I woke one night to a commotion in the bathroom. I tried not to listen, but things got pretty heated. I silently willed them to keep it down in case my sisters might hear, being too young to comprehend it. I'd never heard them so angry: banging, slamming cupboard doors and through the din my mother threatening to leave. I pulled the covers over my head and cried myself to sleep.

The next morning was Saturday and no school. I tiptoed through the house to the kitchen. Mum and Dad's bedroom door was open and the bed was made. There was a thick silence, like treacle. I purposefully banged around making breakfast, petrified. It would be at least an hour before Sarah and Claire emerged from their room, but they said nothing. Nor Richard when he eventually joined us.

Dad's office door was closed and we didn't see him until the afternoon. He came into the lounge and sat down, fidgeting with his wristwatch.

'Hey children,' he said, then paused. My heart was thumping so hard I thought they might hear it. 'Mum's gone to stay with Grans and Gramps for a few days.' He looked at each of us in turn. 'She's fine,' he smiled. 'She just needs a break.'

'When will she be back?' Sarah asked.

'I'm not sure. Hopefully it's just a few days.' Hopefully. The word hit me like a freight train. I desperately wanted to cry.

'If she's with Grans and Gramps, can't we go and see her?' It was Claire, just seven.

'No, darling.' My father reached out and stroked her white-blonde hair. 'I think it's best if we leave Mum in peace for a while.' Claire looked perplexed. 'She'll come back when she's ready.' The rest of the talk was about mucking together to make sure the household chores got done, but I'd already tuned out.

She did come back, four days later and it's still the happiest day of my life. I made sure to give her an extra big squeeze and told her I loved her. 'Thanks for coming back, Mum,' I said. She looked at me quizzically.

'I was always coming back,' she smiled. There was a softness about her that I hadn't seen before. A peacefulness, like she'd exorcised her demons.

I prayed on my knees that night. Normally as a 12-year-old, I'd just do it in bed but when it was warranted I would go down. I thanked God on repeat. I knew he had a hand in it, even then. It's what we'd been taught after all and what we saw our parents do, but it was rare that I felt it.

Mum undoubtedly loved Dad and when things got tough, leaving was complicated. She'd made the lifelong commitment to the church as much as to him and was determined to live up to her promise. In those days divorce was still a big deal, especially for a community figurehead. Family aside, it would have been devastating for his ministry.

But while she toughed it out willingly, the strain of it all was at times immense. And when she tried to bring things up, as soon as she raised her voice Dad withdrew, accusing her of shouting at him, just like his mother had. So they could never have a constructive argument and nothing got dealt with.

Mum was forced to be tenacious, to reshape the very mould of her. She learned to be social, even though friendships in the parish were largely superficial and time to nurture one outside of it non-existent. Despite her best efforts, in the vortex of parish life she often found herself entirely alone and as young children we were the welcome recipients of her affection.

One thing that flowed in abundance in our humble rectory house was love – neither Dad's absence nor the demands of the church would ever change that. It's what I admire most about them now and as children we could not have wished for more. But what I most admired about them then was their dogged commitment to the Struggle:

By the mid 1970's when I was born, St George's Cathedral in Cape Town had become the focal point of the church's opposition movement, a safe haven where Christians from all denominations could unite in the fight for racial justice. Congregants who spilled into the streets after Sunday Eucharist would often be greeted by the Special Branch with water cannons at the ready. A tactical unit of the South African Police Force,

Special Branch's sole mission was to suppress anti-apartheid activism. They acted with impunity, with widespread torture, detention and assassinations swept under its blood-stained carpet.

From St George's Cathedral, the bishops and clergy would frequently march arm in arm, their black and white cassocks flowing in the stiff Cape southeaster. This activism was as calculated as it was noble, government attacks on clergy attracting considerably greater public ire. They filed down Queen Victoria Street towards District Six chanting '*Apartheid won't live forever but we will – bring back free will!*'

As a young child the scenes were preserved in my mind's eye like a grainy documentary, but I don't recall any of my father's arrests. He describes them as nothing more than a show of force, but each time he tells the stories it's like he's reliving the claustrophobic journeys being crammed in the back of over-crowded police vans and the anxious hours spent with his brother Christopher in the holding cells of Caledon Square police headquarters.

It was all just mind-games on the part of the State, ploys to disperse the crowds and strike fear into their leaders. But for others, the perils were a lot more severe. Father Michael Lapsley was an Anglican priest and a staunch social justice activist. In 1990, the year Nelson Mandela walked as a free man, Father Michael was sent a letter bomb from the Civil Cooperation Bureau, a covert arm of Special Branch.

Hidden inside a Christian magazine, the bomb relieved him of both hands and the sight of his left eye. It was a desperate act meant to instil fear in the hearts of those who would oppose the system. Instead, it caused the State more harm than good and it served as another nail in apartheid's coffin.

While I was too young to properly grasp its significance, I was in awe of my parents during that time because they stood up for what they believed. They marched against the oppressors of those not treated as equals. They marched for the freedom of ordinary people to have the right to live ordinary lives. Nothing was more sacred than free will and they could simply not allow such evil to prevail.

Were it not for the active role they played in the Struggle, as children we might well have considered apartheid to be ordinary. It was all we'd ever known and the state-run South African Broadcasting Corporation (SABC) was a well-oiled propaganda machine. Broadcast in different languages, the SABC was the only source of news for many people. Mobile phones, internet and social media didn't exist and most people didn't even own a television.

What little they did hear over the radio was heavily censored. The State took the truth, funnelled it into a giant mincer, added their secret herbs and spices and ground it into palatable deception, hooves and all. Then they stuffed it into pig's intestinal casings so the nation could swallow it in back yard braais while drinking themselves into oblivion.

When you're on the white side of apartheid it's easier not to question, but ride the wave and perhaps even ignore it because it's convenient. We were never allowed to feel entitled, Mum and Dad made sure of that. While our circumstances didn't exactly afford us a sense of privilege, we were constantly reminded of how fortunate we were.

I have also subsequently come to realise that how I felt about it all was quite irrelevant. It was those born on the wrong side of a rotten system that were treated like third-class citizens. They were the ones that had been dealt the lousy hand, not offered the same opportunities, stuck in perpetual degradation in a system that transgressed their basic human rights. No amount of empathy from white people would ever change that and to think otherwise was futile.

Watching Nelson Mandela walk away a free man from Robben Island on 11 February 1990 was exhilarating. We were a nation steeped in hope. As whites opposing the system, we hoped that we could all unite as one people, finally equal in peace and prosperity. Everyone else just hoped it would change their circumstances. More than thirty years later, most South Africans are still hoping for the same things, only I'm now hoping from afar and I no longer get to be reminded.

I can only imagine how momentous Mandela's release might have felt for leaders of the church. People like Anglican Archbishop Desmond Tutu, the leader of the Methodist Church, Peter Storey and Michael Lapsley, the latter who remains an active priest at 73, preaching with the Bible held aloft in his steel callipers.

Father Basil van Rensburg, too, the priest at Holy Cross Roman Catholic Church in District Six, who used to march carrying a small suitcase with some toiletries and a Bible in it, in case he was arrested. He mobilised public opinion against District Six's forced removal programme so successfully that it took 14 years for the government to finish the job. And by the time the last home was destroyed, international condemnation was so widespread and that in the end most of it was left undeveloped.

When I ask my father about the church's role in dismantling apartheid, he says it couldn't have done any more, short of initiating non-peaceful protest. He says that the church can hold its head high and that the nation needed to apologise to people like Desmond Tutu. Apt, given it was Desmond Tutu's role as head of the Truth and Reconciliation Commission to get everyone else to apologise to one another.

But South Africa's reconciliation has also been the greatest test of Dad's ministry. He talks about one of Cape Town's most notorious gangsters Rashied Staggie, who became a born-again Christian. As head of the Hard Livings gang, he was responsible for countless murders, terrorising the Manenberg community against his rival The Americans gang. While the drug rings he brought to the streets are still killing children today, he gets to walk free because he's sorry. Because he said he had no choice but to kill in order to stay alive.

'Forgiving people is the hardest part about being a Christian leader,' my father says. 'The scripture says forgiveness is total, but people like Staggie have left such a trail of devastation. When is forgiveness total?' I share his view that only people who truly repent can be worthy of forgiveness.

He thinks the cross is missing from too many churches today. That's what it's all about, after all – the forgiveness of sins. There has to be recognition of remorse. Staggie started a church of his own, to help reform gangsters. There is surely some merit in that. But sympathies run thin, especially among the families of those he's killed.

3
Like father ...

Anthony Peter Gregorowski was born in Okiep, South Africa's oldest mining town. Set in the country's remote north-west region of Namaqualand, Scottish explorer James Alexander discovered copper there in 1855, quickly transforming the outpost into the world's richest copper mine. Prospectors, miners and speculators flocked there in droves, the town blossoming like the spring flowers that today remain its only tourist attraction.

By the time my father was born in December 1943, Okiep was a shadow of its former self. The only remnants of its glory days were a smokestack, Corning pumphouse and two giant holes in the ground that the members of Okiep Bowls Club swear you can see from space.

It was in 1941 that his father, the Reverend William Gregorowski had been stationed with his young wife Doris and their two young sons, Christopher and Paul at St Augustine's, the town's only Anglican church. My father would be the last in a line of three boys, followed by their only sister, Cait.

Proffering none of the trappings of a leafy suburban neighbourhood, the young Gregorowski children were left to amuse themselves in Okiep's stark and desolate surrounds, which sadly also came to symbolise life inside the walls of the humble rectory.

Father William Gregorowski, or Willy as he was known to close friends and parishioners, was a man of few words but fierce conviction. He ruled with an iron fist, conducting himself with an authority far more suited to the pulpit than his burgeoning family.

Willy had been an actuary by profession but got the calling to be a priest in his 30s. So he left for England to study theology, where he met and married Doris Skinner before escaping home as the winds of war swept Britain. Doris was cut from equally rigid cloth and both were products of an era in which the outward expression of emotion was not only considered socially taboo, but also a sign of weakness, leaving their rectory devoid of any form of affection, either verbal or physical.

Dad describes a bright autumn afternoon arriving at Cape Town train station after serving nine months of military service. He'd been stationed in Bethlehem, in the austere Orange Free State mining community and not the birthplace of Jesus.

No sooner had he stepped off the steam train and without so much as a 'hello' or a hug, Willy and Doris informed him he'd be shipped off to Grahamstown University for five years, 800 kilometres away. They had leveraged their standing with the church to secure free tuition at the country's pre-eminent theological college and simply could not contain their exuberance.

Buried deep in the bottom drawer of his desk is a pile of letters from when he lived away from home. They're addressed 'To my dearest parents' and convey nothing in the way of sentiment or words of affection. To this day he won't read them for fear of reopening old wounds.

'It may be unjust to them, but I didn't have the relationship I so wanted with my parents that I now have with my own children,' he told me. His diplomacy, even though they're no longer with us, speaks volumes of his character. And the relationships we enjoy as a family have undoubtedly formed the bedrock of our own sturdy characters.

For that alone, we are forever in our parents' debt: for our first-class educations, too, which came at no small cost. An all-boys institution widely known for its academic and sporting prowess, Diocesan College, or 'Bishops' as it was widely known, drew the esteem of Cape Town's most well-to-do and upstanding citizens. Richard and I found ourselves there not because we mixed in such circles but because of its links to the Anglican Diocese, our tuition heavily subsidised.

With Dad and his brothers all Bishops alumni, sending us there would also fulfil a long-held desire to give his boys the same education they so greatly cherished. And seeing us follow in his footsteps through its pristine halls would more than warrant the enormous personal sacrifice, even with all the assistance.

He is the first to admit that funding four children through school and university was a small miracle. 'If you had asked at the beginning of my ministry, I would have said absolutely impossible,' he smiles. 'But the scriptures say, if you tithe to God, he will open the windows of heaven and bless you.' Yet 50 years later he still wears his own perceived inability to provide for us like a yoke around his neck, wondering whether they could have done more.

It pains me deeply, especially given the head start the Bishops education has given me in life. What I only fully appreciated later, though, was what it represented at the time: an oasis in the quagmire of apartheid. As a private school, coloured and black students were permitted to attend, although there weren't many for economic reasons and a good proportion of those there were on scholarships.

But it meant that walking through its expansive grounds and running out on the rugby pitches, we didn't have to succumb to the apartheid system's inadequacies. We ran shoulder to shoulder with children of all colours under a common banner and with a common purpose, to become smarter, better, well-rounded humans. This to me was a delight. It represented a thread of defiance and until we passed through the school gates at the end of each day, we could revel in being untouchable by the State.

Doing my small part in this way allowed me to feel closer to my parents, while sharing many Saturday mornings watching Bishops rugby strengthened the bonds in my relationship with Dad. Understanding the lack of affection he and his three siblings endured and that we bore the same rebellious yolk has only instilled in me greater empathy for him. It also helped to curb my bitterness about our restrictive upbringing.

We understand each other and my respect runs deep. As a man of the cloth, he was always on parade, setting an example to his diocese, community and parish. But beneath the cassock he was our father first and foremost. Despite the sacrifices, he wouldn't change a thing given the chance.

Being shipped off to Grahamstown would prove exactly what he needed to be a true servant of the country's abandoned people. It was during this time he was first exposed to South Africa's slums, known as 'townships'. Sporting a cassock and dog collar, he'd ride in the front of St John's Ambulance to help treat burn victims and malnourished children. Many suffered from kwashiorkor owing to a severe lack of nutrition and protein in their diets, ironically causing the liver to swell so much that they looked overweight. But it was a deadly affliction and visiting once a week was enough only to treat the symptoms of a few. Poverty, it seemed, would prove far too skilled a huntsman.

Winter nights in the Eastern Cape townships were bitterly cold and most people lived in huts made of wood offcuts and sheets of corrugated iron. Fires were the only way to keep warm, while paraffin lamps were used for light, so blazes broke out with alarming frequency. Each took more than its fair share of homes before being brought under control, one bucket of water from the communal tap at a time, when the water was running.

This the Grahamstown Fire Department could only watch from the periphery as there was no way to get through or past the connected shacks in fire tenders. And it was among the smouldering ruins that Dad would carry out his gauze and salve ministry.

Whether or not he was ever in harm's way, he wouldn't have known it. Renowned churchgoers, most township residents trekked for hours each Sunday to their nearest place of worship, while their close-knit communities afforded visiting priests a level of protection. Perhaps emboldened by this unspoken pact or just because of his youthful exuberance, Dad came to really understand the plight of his country and develop a deep empathy that would endear him to so many of its people.

God calling

It was a love affair that would culminate in the pews of St Aidan's parish in Lansdowne, where we moved after leaving Bredasdorp. Having been the only English-speaking kids in an Afrikaans school, the government decreed that Richard and I could no longer attend Bredasdorp Laerskool, so we were shipped off to Bishops Preparatory School where we boarded until Dad could relocate to Cape Town.

Lansdowne wasn't exactly one of the city's most salubrious suburbs, but it was close enough to Bishops and the girls' schools to make it work, while Dad's growing responsibilities as archdeacon meant more and more trips into Cape Town. So in 1984 we packed our bags once more and moved into a compact flat-roofed, black burglar-barred house at the bottom of St Aidan's Road. It was to be our home for the next eleven years.

The garden was surrounded by a pre-cast wall, beyond which sprawled a sandy-brown field criss-crossed with footpaths and litter, like a Christmas tree in February. The footpaths converged on a railway station on the other side of which was one of Cape Town's most notorious gangland estates. Flanking the other sides of our property were a parking lot and liquor store warehouse, perfect havens for our homeless.

Tucked behind a garage was a second entrance to the house leading into Dad's office. It was in this little enclosure when returning from school one afternoon that I found two homeless people straddling each other on the doorstep, all discarded clothing and toothless exuberance. The air hung thick with methylated spirits.

Being just eleven at the time, these images will never leave me. But it taught me that we are all human and prone to the same desires and emotions. I wondered then how humiliating it may have been for them, having nowhere to go for even their most private moments. Or whether they'd remember it at all. Regardless, the next time one of the couple knocked at our door for food, I made them a sandwich far more willingly.

But these were just our external trappings that in no way represented the St Aidan's community. School teachers, clerks, council workers and carers, they were people of limited means but blessed with an abundance of spirit. And each Sunday behind the closed doors of their hexagonal house of God there was no discontent, just friends and neighbours standing together in praise, hands upraised to the melodies of the three-piece corner band. It gave me my first real sense of the power of the Holy Spirit at work and it was almost tangible.

Among St Aidan's most dedicated parishioners was Cathy Whiteman. With all four children old enough to fend for themselves, she'd returned to Cape Town the year before I left for boarding school and then lived with her cousin, husband and their two teenage children in a tiny house on the 'other' side of the Lansdowne tracks. When Dad was transferred there, I thought it nothing more than a wonderful coincidence, but now, of course, I know there is no such thing.

In exchange for her meagre State pension, Cathy shared their family meals and was given a room just large enough for a single bed and bedside table, where her Bible took pride of place. While she could, she still read the scriptures morning and night, but as her cataracts grew worse even this simple pleasure was denied her.

Attending church twice a week, therefore, when she could get a ride, was what she looked forward to most, especially on the

Sundays Mum invited her to lunch. Ever prim in a floral dress and white cardigan, soft grey hair neatly combed, she'd sit in the corner chair of our sitting room and revel in being reunited with her family. Mum would make ox tongue, her favourite, which we gladly tolerated for the sake of her company. And when it came to saying goodbye, Cathy did all she could to hide the tears.

As our adolescent years advanced, weeks would go by without seeing her. When I was old enough to drive, I'd take her for occasional outings, perhaps a stroll in Kirstenbosch Gardens or just for scones and tea. She was in her late seventies with limited mobility, so these were labours of love and helping her back through the rusted gate at the end of their sandy yard I felt the pangs of guilt. Guilt for not taking her out more often and not having the means to provide her a better life. Even when pushing a few notes into her pocket, I knew they'd be a household contribution or pilfered by her cousin's son to fund his ice addiction.

It pained me deeply that someone with such an abundant love and consummate dedication to God could have so little. The irony of course is that I understand now she had everything she needed all along. 'Matthew, Jesus loves you. That is all that matters,' she used to say. She lived each mundane day to its fullest in the knowledge that God was alive in her. In this she was at peace and I had no right to wish her a better life.

In this regard, Cathy was not alone. While no-one I know has lived such a model existence, through Dad's ministry I knew plenty of people who lived each day complete and happy in the love of God. It has always given me great comfort that even if there is no God –and when our days draw to a close there really is nothing more – the fulfilment that faith alone has provided to so many that have so little is surely reason enough to endorse it.

Cathy was 83 when she died. In her final months she sat quietly in a soulless, unsanitary nursing home in Mitchells Plain on the Cape Flats. Adjacent to Cape Town's largest township, Khayelitsha, it was a stone's throw from where the good people of District and many of Cathy's friends had been relocated. Her eyesight was too poor to read her Bible or see anything out of the small window of her solitary room. She had few visitors other than our family, Mum and Dad once picking up scabies after visiting.

By then I had long finished university and left South Africa, my travels setting me on a different course. It meant I was the only member of my immediate family unable to be there at the end, so I had to say goodbye on a mobile phone that Mum held to Cathy's ear. She seemed to be holding on for something, so I told her it was okay to let go, that she would soon be with Jesus where she belonged. After hanging up I crumpled to the floor and wept for what seemed an eternity. She died the next day.

Recalling that moment, my sister Sarah remarked that I was lucky not to have been there. She will never forget the image of Cathy looking so frail and gaunt, her once pristine hair matted and greasy, bathed in an odour of death. For this I am truly thankful, my lasting memories of Cathy Whiteman being of her sitting in the corner of our family home with her soft dark eyes, silk-white hair and bashful smile. Graceful, angelic and content.

I still think of her often. She remains one of my most faithful spiritual guides and for all humanity she surely remains an example. I am also grateful to my parents for their generosity in taking Cathy in, in helping to give her a sense of purpose beyond her faith. And it was only in my coming of age during those Lansdowne years that I really came to understand the life of service they led and the love they earnt from all those receiving their unwavering charity.

It was also there that I really came to admire Dad's preaching. He spoke with authority and authenticity, while his infectious charm and razor-sharp wit defined him. In the eyes of the parish, he was a veritable rock star. Each Saturday night he would disappear into his study to read the scriptures and pray. By sunrise he was gone, sermon neatly folded into his King James Bible. There was always a swelling in my chest when he stepped into the pulpit or perhaps I just sensed his anxiety. But as soon as he started speaking, he had us all eating from the palm of his hand.

With this growing adoration of Dad as a preacher and community figurehead it would have been easy for me to follow in his footsteps, yet the idea could not have felt more foreign. The calling to be a priest is not something that one volunteers, nor necessarily wishes for. Dad got the nod in his penultimate year of school and never looked back. From then on, his path was clearly laid out, his dedication to God and church unwavering.

I have asked him more than once about this experience and the answer was simple. God called to him in his heart. The yearning to bestow on others the teachings of the Christian faith was so overwhelming that there was simply no alternative. In a number of ways, I always envied him for that. And it spurred in me a deep desire to understand not just my father the man, but my father the man of God.

I needed to know in my own heart what it was that he felt. It was exactly because I saw God touch the lives of so many through

Dad's ministry that I needed to experience it for myself. And it was precisely because of all the hardships we had to endure as a family that I needed to know how he could willingly sacrifice so much for the service of others.

My path to understanding myself lay in understanding Dad's relationship with God. The only way I'd ever perceived that was through Jesus Christ and the Christian church, the same path trodden by Dad and his father. But that was never my own lived experience. While I undoubtedly witnessed the Holy Spirit at work in the aisles of All Saints in Bredasdorp and St Aidan's in Lansdowne, God didn't come to my door or answer my prayers. I needed to find God in my own way. And even then, I sensed that it was only in this way that I could truly find peace.

Nowadays, I see Dad's hands every day. Above all else, it is his hands that I've inherited. They are a constant reminder of where I come from and of the responsibility that comes from living in his example. I take enormous pride in knowing it is my father's hands that write these words, one more sermon, years in the making.

He shared with me recently that he still gets anxious before stepping up into the pulpit, even after 50 years of ministry. It's another trait I've inherited and how apt that it's what led to the opening of my own spiritual doorway all these years later. To the beginning of a journey which will see me pick up the mantle of service to others, of spreading the word, just in my own nuanced way – no need for a cassock or dog collar.

Being the son of a preacher man has certainly not been an easy ride. But the preacher man's shoes are mighty comfortable. And they are lined with good intent.

4
Forging a new path

It was in those Lansdowne years that I also really came to admire Mum. Mostly it was for managing two physically strong boys and placating two teenage girls, all while capturing the hearts and minds of all those in the parishes she served. She had a knack for cutting us down to size, yet you always knew it was out of love. Nothing is more disarming.

She was a mother figure above all else and not just to us children. She took each of our domestic workers under her wing, too, she befriended them and treated them as equals. This was undoubtedly the product of her own struggle growing up in the early days of apartheid. When she'd ask her parents about it, the answer was always the same. 'It's just the way it is. It's the law.' Perhaps it's why Mum and Dad were always so open with us about it, about how it made them feel.

When she found things all too much, she did courses on managing troubled teenagers, still always second guessing herself whether she was doing things the right way. Again, it was borne of her own perceived inadequacies. She'd been sickly as a child and had to drink rice water instead of milk, her Mum feeding her tonics to compensate. She became overweight, severely knocking her confidence while hampering her prospects as a talented ballerina. But as is her nature she persevered and her name remains engraved on several trophies.

Throughout school she was a bright student and desperately wanted to go to university, but despite stellar grades her parents considered home-making a far more suitable pastime for their two attractive daughters. And after meeting Dad as a young teenager, there was a long hiatus until their wedding at 21, her golden years spent waiting for a letter, phone call or the occasional visit.

Mum's parents were deeply religious and at school she was taught by nuns. It made her decision to marry a clergyman a very natural one, especially given their strong endorsement. And despite all the sacrifices, it has given her lifelong fulfilment beyond what she could have hoped to gain from any profession. Without her support, Dad would never have been able to carry out his ministry as he did, a ministry she was very much a part of. She harbours no regrets, but there is still part of her, and me, that wonders what may have been.

She had her own spiritual battles along the way, too. When things at home were tough she tried searching for her own path to a deeper fulfilment. She signed up at the Department of Spirituality, where she learned to experience God in a more personal way, to witness God being spoken about in a way she had never heard before. She practised meditation, worshipped with different forms of music and shared stories and experiences with others looking for their own answers. These are parallels with my own journey I have discovered much later in life and like it was for me, this was a seminal time in the evolution of her faith. Her relationship with God blossomed and she came to understand that we all need to be examples for others. It's what she still strives for every day.

It also reinvigorated her sense of purpose in her involvement with the Church and even in retirement her commitment remains unwavering. Given the choice she would do it all again, but now she also has friendships outside the church that she's had the time to nurture. And that peacefulness I saw in her that day she came back to us, remains.

In her later years Mum has undoubtedly mellowed and while the relationship I have with her has never been more wholesome, we certainly had our moments during my troubled teens. It was also during those Lansdowne years that I hit the height of my rebellion. The standards of behaviour expected of us under the vicar's roof left little room for interpretation and much to Mum and Dad's dismay I developed a deep disrespect for authority.

At first, we clashed over everything from parental-guidance rated movies to hairstyles, but later I'd start skipping school, a red rag for parents breaking their backs to fund our first-rate educations. I ran away, too, once hitchhiking a two-hour ride back to Cape Town from our family's holiday home up the east coast. I just couldn't stand being around them.

Then came my introduction to girls, cigarettes and alcohol, like a crash test dummy careering into adolescence. I started hitting bars and nightclubs, frequently staying with friends whose parents were more liberal. But it wasn't enough to protect me from my own exploits. I was frequently grounded, sometimes cutting deals with Mum to keep Dad from finding out, like when I was caught smoking pot while still at school. Unbeknown to all of us at the time, it would be the start of a long love affair with Mary Jane that I would only shake when entering corporate life.

In many ways these were just normal pitfalls of a misguided youth. But there was vandalism, too, senseless smashing of public property and breaking into other neighbourhood schools, just for the thrill of it. Of course, alcohol played a part but there was no excuse.

I've often reflected on why I did these things given the intense anxiety of being caught. In Dad's eyes these deeds would have been intolerable, yet I flaunted them with abandon. Perhaps they were the product of frustration, of an inability to express myself in a way that was acceptable, or they were a blatant rebellion against claustrophobia, like a caged gorilla, or a fish always out of water.

Whatever my motivations, over the years I tested Dad's resolve more frequently than I ever had the right to. And to his credit, despite the frustrations, his patience prevailed. He was as consistent in his admonishment as in his absolution. Perhaps he sympathised because of our affinity, realised or not. Perhaps it was just because he's a good man, because he is a man of God.

But there were times when I pushed the boundaries too far, blatantly disrespecting the values he and Mum had worked so hard to instil in us, never more so than as a 17-year-old fresh out of high school.

I took a gap year before university to save money for a car, landing a job as a door-to-door salesman flogging cheap Chinese junk to charitable shopkeepers and housewives. I'd leave home at six o'clock in the morning and get back to find my dinner in the warming drawer. It was hard work but made more tolerable by a beautiful dark-skinned colleague, Carmella and when the flirting hit fever pitch there was only one thing on my mind. The only issue was that her house was a 45-minute drive away while mine was a 15-minute walk. So I convinced her to come to the rectory after work and sneak in through my outside bedroom door.

As far as plans go it was foolproof. I told my parents I was heading straight for bed, then letting her in via the garden gate, I locked both bedroom doors and put on my favourite Def Leopard tape to drown out the noise.

It might have worked, too, had it not been for my curious 11-year-old sister. When Claire rapped on my door the first time, I reassured the poor girl underneath me that my sister would go away. Even when she came knocking a second time and called out 'Matthew' I simply put a finger to her lips and kept going, such was the excitement building in my youthful loins.

It was only when my mother arrived a few minutes later that the gravity of the situation took hold. Only by this stage any sense or sensibility had been completely paralysed by a thundering climax. And it was only in the ensuing glow, as we lay there panting that reality dawned in the shape of a small body creeping through my fanlight window. In the shadows I saw it reach down and unlock the door from the inside before I even had time to react.

It's in situations like these that you can never quite predict how you'll respond. Jumping out of bed, pulling the covers over my petrified partner and diving under the desk might not have been everyone's course of action, but it seemed entirely logical at the time. And when the vicar stormed in, hit the light switch and stood momentarily scanning the room, it's unclear to me what thoughts might have been racing through my mind.

What I do recall is feeling decidedly grave when he ripped off the covers, only to find a strange lady preserving what modesty she could with her violently shaking arms. And knowing that things had gone entirely sideways when both sisters followed him into the room as I cowered naked under the desk, prophylactic still dangling limply like a wounded soldier.

It was then the music stopped.

'Where's Matthew?' bellowed my father in a tone I've never had the displeasure of hearing since.

'I don't know,' was all Carmella could offer, evidently on the verge of tears.

From the pause that ensued I knew my father's attention had finally turned to the gap beneath my desk. Such gargantuan moments can often create distortions in time and in my life to date there has never been a longer one, although it might well have only been a second or two. It was certainly long enough for the nausea to take hold.

'Damn it, why didn't you answer the door?' echoed through my now throbbing head as he pounded his fist on the desk. There was nothing to do but sink my head deeper into my hands, until all that was left was silence.

We dressed. I apologised. She cried. Then we walked down the hall past my siblings' closed doors to join Mum and Dad in the sitting room. To say the conversation was awkward would be an understatement, although it has long since been erased from my memory in self-preservation. Worse, though, was the drive home. Not yet old enough for a full licence, my father had to accompany us to Carmella's house. Not a single word was spoken and on that hour and a half journey I lived a lifetime of self-admonishment. How could I be so brazenly disrespectful? How could I be such a disappointment to the two people who had worked so tirelessly to set me on a wiser path? And had Dad not been in the seat next to me, I might well have more than fantasised about swerving into oncoming headlights.

There were several lines crossed that night, not least of which was having sex before marriage. The worst part, though, was that they thought I was committing suicide, surely any parent's greatest fear. And if I put myself in their shoes it's easy to see how they got there. If only I had answered the door, although I've never known hindsight to comfort anyone.

Rather, it would be a moment I'd relive many times in introspection, often as I've reflected on why it is so painful growing up and why it's so hard for us to accept our parents when in time we come to realise they are just good people doing their best for us.

The answer is that there's a lesson in honesty wrapped up in that smorgasbord of screw-ups and it's only in lived experiences and the self-reflection that follows that we really learn the most about ourselves. It's simple cause and effect and were I given the opportunity, like Mum and Dad, I wouldn't change a thing.

I'm not sure how long it took to rebuild their trust after that night and we've never spoken about it since, nor have I ever apologised for my behaviour. But there is a deep mutual understanding between us that we all did our best and that's surely all any of us could ask for.

While Dad often preferred blissful naïveté, I always had the sense that Mum knew more than she let on about what we got up to as children. Some things, though, are better left unsaid and their contentment comes from seeing all of us turn out to be fundamentally wholesome people.

What I do know, above all else, is that we got there because of them after being the subjects of copious prayer. There have been too many incidents, too many close calls, times when I haven't deserved to come out the other end intact. But I did and as I have only come to appreciate along my own spiritual journey, there is no such thing as luck. Now, all I can do is live by their example and be the same for others, just as Mum taught us.

5
Death becomes you

There were elements of Dad's ministry that were undoubtedly confronting. Our domestic worker in Bredasdorp, Betty, called him in a panic one afternoon. *'Vader, daar's 'n tokolosh in die huis, maak gou, 'seblief.'* (Father, there's a tokolosh in the house, please hurry). When we got to her house in the onderdorp she was shaking, no sign of her trademark toothless smile.

The tokolosh is an evil, dwarf-like spirit originating from Zulu and Xhosa mythology and is feared by many South African communities. It is believed to be conjured by malicious people wanting to inflict harm on others and only visible to children. She said it was being chased by the neighbourhood kids and had run inside her house, so Dad performed the exorcism and Betty had a whisky.

But there had been numerous adult sightings of the tokolosh, too, including by Dad's secretary, Maria. She'd arrived at the parish office ashen-faced one morning. Crossing a field on her usual route to the train station, she saw a small, hunched man dressed in black walking a few feet ahead of her. But no sooner had she spotted him than he darted off and disappeared into a tree stump. It was only then that she realised what it was.

That day in the onderdorp was one of many rituals Dad would conduct alone. The Bishop's permission was usually required for exorcisms but in rural South Africa that wasn't always practical.

The exorcisms concerned places where he'd often sense an uncomfortable presence and sometimes he'd experience it with people too. But the most daunting time was with a young boy in Lansdowne who woke up to fires burning in his bedroom. After the ceremony of prayers and holy water, Dad left a crucifix on the boy's bookcase. The fires never returned.

These were events that intrigued me as a boy and have evolved over the years to become my single greatest fascination.

Growing up in the confines of Christianity raised more questions than answers. I needed to understand the fundamental tenets of religion and not just learn them, none more so than the line between life and death, between our perceived world and what lies beyond it.

Death had always been part of Dad's ministry. Not just the funerals but comforting those who were near to it and consoling their loved ones. My grandparents have passed away, but I wasn't especially close to any of them. In fact, it was only as Willy and Doris both neared death that I saw them at their most real and vulnerable for the first time. I wonder whether Dad felt the same way.

My own first real encounter with death came while I was at Bishops. Hamilton Mvelase was a bright young man, one of just a handful of black students on the school's scholarship programme. At 18, it was his third year as a live-in boarder and it was our penultimate before graduating.

On a bright Sunday morning like any other, Hamilton deliberated between taking the train home to see his family and staying in bed. Roping in his close friend Bennett Kangisa, they set off for the township of Gugulethu. It was a decision that would prove fatal.

Crossing a field towards his house, Hamilton was stabbed multiple times by a random attacker. The perpetrator first set on Bennett and when Hamilton tried to intervene, the attacker turned on him. Bennett Kangisa is alive and well today, but the news of Hamilton's untimely death shook our school to the core. The injustice of such a talented and lively, humble boy falling victim to senseless violence was as infuriating as it was confronting. The very place from which his privileged education was to set him free, swallowed him whole, as if in spite. It was a tragedy that left us all reeling, less for our own sadness and more for the promising future so brutally stolen.

Our collective anger reverberated all the way to the Bishops chaplain, Reverend Michael Bands, who at the memorial service grimly declared 'To say what happened to Hamilton was God's will is absolute rubbish. I say that with all the conviction of my being.'

Perhaps blaming the establishment provided him comfort, but it was the first time I'd heard a man of the cloth speak with such emotion against the teachings of the church. It was refreshing and reminded me that under every cassock is just a man who sees and feels as we do. I always respected him for that.

How many of us are brought to our knees when we couldn't see God's will in the senseless death of someone we loved? And how often are we engulfed by a futile rage at the carelessness of forces and people beyond our control?

Hamilton wasn't a close friend. We attended a few classes together and played on the same rugby team. But his death left its mark and we all mourned him in our own way.

It would prove to be a taste of things to come, only far closer to home and a tragedy that has had the single most profound impact on my life.

This one tore open my heart and shattered the boundaries of my Christian education, ultimately setting me on the spiritual path I still find myself on 30 years later.

Michael John Fisher died on 20 September, 1994. He was 19 and one of my closest friends.

Of our close-knit group of school friends Mike was physically the most imposing. As a seasoned water polo player, he was tall and broad shouldered, yet he had a gentle and easy manner. Behind lively brown eyes was an old soul, always seeking the good in people. It meant others were naturally drawn to him despite his innate shyness. He was an all-round good human and wonderful friend, the kind of guy you wanted your daughter to bring home. But it is his infectious laugh I remember most fondly.

So when he bummed a ride home from a party one rainy winter's night and was flung out of the car, our world as we knew it came to a standstill. The last recollection Mike may have had would have been passing out on the back seat as the car raced towards his digs at Stellenbosch University. He would be yet another senseless victim of drink driving. And while the details of the accident were never relayed to us, the driver survived. His life, too, undoubtedly ruined.

The news arrived that Sunday morning and by lunchtime we were all at his bedside in Tygerberg Hospital. The small semi-private room smelled of sterilised bedpans. Tubes ran into his throat and arms. Seeing him lying there so lifeless and debilitated was numbing. We just stared in silence. There is no manual for moments like those, no advice and no warning. The emotions are the most raw you've ever known, but you don't recognise any of them.

I'll always remember the drive home in the back of our Toyota station wagon. The national road from Stellenbosch, which is home to some of the world's most affluent wine farms, is flanked by misery. On both sides tin shacks spill from bloated townships onto the road's grassy verge like an over-squeezed tube of cement crack filler.

We passed by in slow motion as if our brains were having trouble processing information. Not even the desperate plight of these people seemed real, people who have nothing and for whom death is part of their daily existence. I stared at this foreign world without a flicker of emotion, like my capacity to feel anything had been wiped clean. And as I stared ahead at Table Mountain engulfed by thunderclouds, I thought of Hamilton and wondered what his family was doing.

Mike was in a coma for two weeks and we visited most days. At first, we just sat in silence, but we soon found that the only thing to bring us comfort was to speak to him like we always did. Like he was joining in, laughing the way only Mike could.

We talked about what was filling our days and plans for the summer. We cracked jokes about how he was faking it to bunk lectures, told him to hurry up as the prank was getting old. We said how much we missed him and looked forward to hanging out again.

The cruellest part was that after a week he started to show positive signs. There was some movement and he'd responded to his family. We grew ever more hopeful, the nightmare perhaps no more than a scare after all.

So when my father walked into our sitting room that mundane Tuesday evening to deliver the news, the shock was all the more pronounced.

My head sank into my hands and for a while everything went blank. Then it hit me, like a bullet ripping through my chest. I ran to my room at the far end of the house and would have kept going if I could. I was desperate to make it stop but the pain kept coming like a tsunami. And then it all came out, the guttural wailing.

My parents ran after me and tried to provide comfort, but all I wanted was for the earth to swallow me. Nothing made sense anymore and when the tears eventually stopped I wanted to be alone, to sleep.

Each of the mornings that followed was as cruel as the last. Waking just to remember was reliving the pain all over again. But as they days passed, they grew easier and life without Mike went on.

The aftermath passed by in a dream, each important part contingent on letting go. First seeing Mike's family, then talking about the funeral, writing his eulogy. The service at Bishops chapel had standing room only, yet the sound of a pin dropping would have reverberated around its giant white dome.

The tributes were fitting. For our part, while we all had a hand in crafting the words, I was tasked with delivering them. I don't recall what was said, but it felt right and worthy of the man we'd lost far too soon.

For a long time, I thought about Mike every day. I thought about his brother and parents, wondered whether they could ever really be whole again. These days it's infrequent, but when I do think of him it makes me smile. I see those vibrant eyes and hear his laugh. And I take comfort knowing how happy Mike would have been to see how he's shaped my life since. I look forward to thanking him one day, because when we communicated with him that first time, it was he who was thanking us.

I was really taken aback when one of our friends suggested contacting Mike. Sean's mother was a medium and believed it might help us to heal. But this was a concept so foreign to the Christian doctrine ingrained in me from childhood and the mere fact that it may be possible challenged all my logical ideals. I also knew going into it that once I had crossed the line there would be no going back.

But curiosity is a wondrous thing, the desire to explore new possibilities is part of our constitution. Mostly, though, I agreed because I wanted to say hi to my friend.

It was a sunny Saturday afternoon when we gathered at Sean's house. Specks of dust clung to sunbeams striking the polished wooden furniture. We gathered round the dining room table, empty but for a clean note pad and pen next to where Debbie sat. She explained the process in a soothing voice and asked if we had any questions.

Then she picked up the pen and closed her eyes. Sean, Zane and I looked at each other anxiously. Perched on the arm of the sofa I was suddenly aware of my frenetic heartbeat. But it slowed with the passing minutes and the creeping doubt. I hadn't considered that nothing may happen, nor the weight of that disappointment.

Another five minutes passed. Then at the slightest movement of Debbie's hand we all leaned forward, as if rehearsed. There was another long pause, then a quick sidewise swipe. And a second one slightly longer. I had to remember to breathe.

Suddenly, her hand sprung to life. First a series of sideways movements like a heart-rate monitor. The lines became scribbled shapes. Slowly with each stroke of the pen they took on more form and began making recognisable shapes. At first the letters were illegible and jagged. But then, quite effortlessly, the words began to flow across the page as if Mike himself was sitting at the table.

For all Mike's beautiful attributes, handwriting wasn't one of them. His was decidedly unruly, as if he'd majored in doctor's prescriptions. And for those of us who knew him, his handwriting was about as distinctive as a Picasso to seasoned critics. Debbie's hand now floated with consummate ease and the words that spilled across that single sheet of foolscap paper were undoubtedly those of our dear friend.

We sat transfixed, close enough to recognise his hand but too far to make out the words. Sentence after sentence came, each quicker than the last as if he couldn't get it out fast enough. Then just as quickly as they had come to life, they stopped. I desperately wanted to touch Debbie's arm before Mike left, but held back.

Minutes passed, her hand rested quietly on the near-full page. A stillness eclipsed the room as if suspended in time. Slowly Debbie opened her eyes. Then after adjusting to the afternoon light, she looked down at the page and smiled, as if she had no idea what she might find. Then turned to us and said 'Well, it looks like you've had a visitor.'

I choked back the tears. 'Would you like me to read it?' she asked.

Mike greeted us in his usual jovial way. He thanked us for keeping him company in the hospital, making references to our conversations that only someone in the room could have. Then he said 'Please don't ever worry about me. I am in a place more beautiful than you could ever imagine.' He signed off telling us how much he loved us.

Debbie sat in silence while we melted around her. I'd given up holding back, tears flowing freely and dropping onto the wooden floorboards. She handed out tissues and touched my shoulder as she walked past. The door clicked shut behind her and we were alone once more, elated yet stunned, joyful in our sorrow.

I only ever talk about that day when occasion calls for it, part of sharing my own journey to perhaps help others shape theirs. And I know each time Mike is there beside me, giving me his blessing. I have never feared death since that day, in many ways I even look forward to it. That in itself gives me peace, as does knowing I will see my friend again.

I had always adhered to the idea that reuniting with God at the end required living in Christ's example, a fundamental tenet of the Christian faith, but I'd never contemplated the experience of that reunification. The experience that afternoon gave me so much more than simple validation. It enlivened in me not just the idea of experiencing God in that way, but of entirely new possibilities. Like the blinkers of perception had been cast aside and the universe revealed in all its stellar glory.

So when the three of us went to our favourite beachside bar that night to toast Mike and revel in the experience, there was a lightness about me which I'd never known. A lightness that has grown with each step along the new path on which it set me.

6
Touched by an angel

Growing up I'd been determined not to follow in my father's footsteps, just as he had been determined not to follow in Willy's. I was too disillusioned by the financial stress Mum and Dad went through despite their best efforts to hide it, so I took up law instead.

The problem was that half-way through undergrad law I realised it was nothing like the glamorous American legal dramas that had lured me in the first place. And having skipped one too many lectures I was lumped with half a dozen subjects in my final year, which I swatted for in the bedroom of our quiet leafy Pinelands surrounds. It was Dad's last rotation and his first white parish in 35 years of ministry. The spacious rectory was a well-deserved swansong to Mum and Dad's retirement and a home that as adolescent children we remember fondly.

I was stubbing out a cigarette while cramming for my exams when Mum came in with a letter. It was from my brother, Richard. He'd gone to England after the army and wrote of eclectic new friends, a trendy shared digs and bustling London night life. He signed off that he'd be home for Christmas, after which he'd be packing a bag and travelling the world.

I realised that if I passed my exams I could go with him, a vision of an empty road stretching into the distance suddenly appearing through the haze of cigarette smoke. So it was that the university of life would wind me up and set me on my ultimate course. And when we boarded the plane for Australia, the first country on our round-the-world adventure, I had no idea it would be the last time I would live on African soil.

It was then I fell in love with Australia and vowed one day to return. It was also when I met the first – and who may perhaps still be the greatest love of my life – on the Oz Experience bus tour from Sydney to Cairns.

Joining a ragtag of Bondi backpackers, Richard and I realised that the pristine New South Wales coastline was just a by-product for the revellers aboard our avocado-green Coachliner. It was a long way to the northern reaches of Queensland and the distances between stop-offs were so vast that jostling for a seat beside the next potential conquest became as tactical as it was terrifying. Running out of chat five minutes into a five-hour journey can literally break a man.

With the first few stages marked by one fumbling encounter and just four days to go, a Danish goddess with long dark hair and chocolate eyes slipped into the seat next to me. We were just setting off on one the longest stretches of our journey and I'd stopped breathing.

'Hi, I'm Karina.' I stared at her. What the hell was my name? 'You're Matthew, right?' Thank God for her.

'I am. And I'll be your trusted tour guide for the next few hours so please buckle up and make yourself comfortable.' As she laughed I felt my shoulders loosen and the saliva return to my mouth.

Karina was confident but kind and she had a soothing charm and sharp intellect; any intimidation quickly dissolved under the warmth of her smile. But it was her gentle nature and generosity of spirit that ultimately captured my heart that day, wrapped it in cottonwool and changed it forever.

After that I was, quite simply, lost. And for the rest of our Oz Experience I traded tequila-fuelled table dancing and humid hangovers for moonlit beach walks and pillow talk under the stars.

Reluctantly we said goodbye at Mission Beach and as I gave her one last kiss, I slipped a matchbox bearing a picture of Paris, into her hand. It's where we'd agreed to meet again someday, inside the box my only ring bearing an Arabic inscription. I had no idea what it meant, so it came to represent all of our hopes and dreams. And I wanted her never to forget.

It would be more than a year before we met again, only in London and not Paris, but there wasn't a day in between that we hadn't strolled along the deserted beaches of my mind.

Our letters had been sporadic, hampered by my being constantly on the move, so when I plucked up the courage to phone her one dreary winter's afternoon, my heart pounded so hard I feared she might hear it. Two weeks later she stood on my Turnpike Lane doorstep and with that very first smile I was in love all over again.

I frequented low-cost airlines to Copenhagen as much as my leave and budget allowed and in between she graced London with her presence. There was a natural beauty about our union, like snow at Christmas and a bond being fostered I had no idea was possible. There is an inherent peacefulness knowing you will be with someone forever and when you're 24 you never contemplate it ending.

But there's also a beautiful naïveté about such innocence and cynicism is the ugly cousin of experience. What I've learnt since is that most of us grow up as dreamers and grow old as wonderers and that those of us who do become truly wise often only do so through adversity. The ending of Karina's and my world was as sudden as it was surreal, but not before she rewrote my playbook on life, love and reverence.

Studying at Odense University in Denmark she was halfway to becoming a doctor when she signed up for the exchange programme to Harare Central Hospital, with no thought to the conditions she might find in Zimbabwe's destitute capital. She spent a month in its maternity ward in the spring of 1999, before I met her for a sojourn through Southern Africa. I had this obsequious notion I'd need to show her the ways of Africa, help to settle her into its colourful ways and steer her clear of its pitfalls. But on our meeting in Dar es Salaam, as she regaled me with her experiences, I realised it was she who would be teaching me.

Delivering babies on the blood-streaked linoleum floor of an overflowing maternity ward and running out of water for three days is enough to shake even the most seasoned professional. Yet she spoke only of her compassion for these desperate mothers, something I found as endearing as it was extraordinary.

Dar es Salaam's Ubungo Bus Terminal is a sprawling concrete square with a triangular billboard in the centre from which a lone rusted Lucky Strike hoarding dangles precariously. We were headed for Mbeya near the northern Malawi border, some 900 kilometres through central Tanzania.

Muscling our way to the back of the bus, we perched on our backpacks and watched the bus fill with people, chickens and pigs like a giant game of Tetris. With all sixty passengers settled in, our 30-seat tin can finally spluttered through the terminal gate, spewing black diesel clouds in celebration.

The ritual of packing and unpacking was a laboured pastime on each stop of the 14-hour journey, which saw us limp into Mbeya as the day's last light dissolved behind a purple horizon. And with it went any semblance of civility.

Like many African countries, Tanzania is blighted by extreme poverty and before we'd even come to a halt the bus was surrounded. With our backpacks and daypacks tightly strapped, no sooner had we set foot on the tarmac than a hundred-strong horde corralled us away from the safety of prying eyes.

'Hold on,' I shouted locking wrists with Karina. Hands grabbed at every pocket of my packs and dirty slacks, like piranhas on a cadaver. I tried to swivel round and grab her, but the sheer force of the crowd was pinning me sideways. Suddenly there was an orchestrated surge, trying to separate us.

'Don't let go,' Karina cried out. I could only catch glimpses of her through the sea of frantic bodies. Another wave, this time more of them and the momentum was too strong. Karina's wrist slipped from my hand and we spun around as a wall drove between us.

'Shout so I can hear you.' My feet weren't even touching the ground and my arms were pinned, as if in some well-orchestrated manoeuvre. Hands were clawing everywhere and the less they found the more desperate they became, the snarls of the hyenas growing ever louder.

I loved watching nature programmes growing up. While the BBC boycotted South Africa during apartheid, Dad once smuggled in David Attenborough's Life on Earth series after a trip to London. We devoured it in two sittings and I'd been hooked ever since.

The wilds of Africa were my favourite, the Serengeti plains, Okavango Delta and Maasai Mara. Lions taking down wildebeest, a cheetah chasing down a kudu and even packs of wild dogs mauling an unsuspecting impala. But what I loved more than the thrill of the kill was seeing a baby elephant rescued by its crazed mother, or a buffalo dragging a train of lions for the safety of the river. I admired their fight and the ferocity of the sheer will to survive.

'Matt!' Karina's voice was fading. I can only it put down to raw instinct, but as my feet touched the tarmac I abandoned all sense of reason. I clenched my fists and fought through the crowd, sweat-clad bodies twisting in both directions. Then catching sight of her backpack through the steaming dusk I dropped my shoulder and charged forward. I grabbed it with both hands and swung her round. 'Hold on.' Her eyes were wide but steady and clutching my straps she pulled in close. Then using hers as a shield, I drove my legs like pistons on a pumpjack.

Suddenly we broke through the crowd and half stumbled to the ground. Scrambling to our feet, we ran behind a nearby minibus. 'Are you okay?' She was breathing hard but smiling, eyes alight. Then she hugged me. 'This is Africa,' she whispered in my ear.

Through the windows of the Toyota Hiace I looked back towards the bus. The crowd was dispersing as quickly as it had assembled, seeping back into the pores of desperate mother Africa.

'Room?' said a man stepping out from nowhere. I looked up at a set of straight white teeth under a battered fedora. His short-sleeved shirt hung half-unbuttoned from a scraggly frame. Behind him the sky was a wondrous violet.

'You bet,' I smiled back at him.

'Yes, yes, I have good room. You come with me.' He reached for my day pack, still stuck to my chest. I handed it to him gladly.

A Damascus moment

The next morning we arrived at the bus terminal early to make sure we would get tickets. The 10 am bus due for Malawi's Nkhata Bay arrived at just after 3.30 pm so it had been a long wait, the queue in front of a single wooden ticket office becoming something of a social affair.

Sarong-clad, well-endowed women chirped and chatted while their half-naked children played with wild berries in the dust. The two *msungus* (colloquial Swahili term for white people) were undoubtedly a topic of much debate and we were glad to be their source of amusement.

But when the concertina door of the battered coach slammed open and a lone conductor stepped into the clearing, any semblance of order disappeared in a cloud of dust. Everyone descended on him with alarming dexterity, crumpled bills shoved frantically in his direction while he dished out bits of paper and change from the coin dispenser around his waist.

Karina was up like a jackrabbit, shouting for me to bring the packs. I watched in awe as she sliced through the throng to appear right in front of the diminutive man and then emerged triumphant with two bits of paper. 'It's easy when you know the system,' she laughed. I think I fell in love with her all over again that day. Perhaps a few times.

The north of Malawi is not renowned for its infrastructure. Seasonal rains wash away the softer layers of dirt from its gravel roads, leaving them scarred and potholed. The bare wooden seats on which we hugged our knees offered little in the way of protection. And it was suddenly quite apparent how our more well-endowed fellow travellers made it through these arduous journeys.

This time the pens of chickens were strung up on the roof, allowing more space for the passengers inside. I gave up counting as every time a different new face popped up, always smiling. When getting a spot on the bus is your only task for the day, it comes with an immense sense of satisfaction.

As the bus jolted over the fourth pothole in as many minutes on our 430-kilometre journey, we knew it would be a test of our resolve. But the mood was jovial and our beast of burden purred along in the burning heat with a full tank of petrol and a song in its heart.

Through the scratched and battered windows, orange scrub and the occasional acacia tree drifted slowly by and as the sun started to drop, it brushed the distant mountains in a light pink hue. It was the serenity of this landscape that had my full attention when the bus suddenly lurched skyward. When it crashed back to the ground, the force was such that we bowed in unison to a crunching, grinding noise below.

I knew instantly it was the gearbox, but only appreciated the severity of our situation when we piled out into the dry heat. It had dropped clean through the chassis and lay covered in dirt as dripping oil filled the foot-long rut it had forged in the road. We were in for a long wait.

The desolate road tapered off in both directions. Karina and I pored over a map in our travel guide but with no idea where we were, it served little purpose. Children were piling sticks and roots to make a fire, while two of the women unstrapped strings of green bananas from underneath the bus. By all appearances they were settling in for the night.

We had no food and had run out of water, so there was little option but to try and walk to the next village. So we loaded up and set off at pace, once again much to the amusement of our fellow passengers. Despite the sun sitting low over the mountains the heat was still stifling. We knew that as soon as it dipped out of sight the temperature would drop rapidly and we needed to arrive before dark, wherever it was we were going to.

The monotonous crunch of gravel underfoot was hypnotic, occasionally broken by the screech of circling hawks. We second-guessed ourselves several times, but with the bus far behind us we decided to stay the course.

In the distance a lone tree cast a spindly shadow across the road and as we approached we saw a figure standing in its shade. At first I thought we must be imagining it, but as we drew nearer it was clearly the outline of a man. He stood with his back to us, small but erect, holding a cane.

We slowed our pace and as we approached he turned towards us. He was elderly, with grey tightly curled hair that cut a stark contrast against his skin and clothes. At first it was just his appearance that reminded me of Archbishop Desmond Tutu. Perhaps it was the pleasantness of his face, or his alluring smile. But it was the similarity in his voice that caused me to stop dead in my tracks. 'Good afternoon,' he beamed.

'Hello, sir,' I said.

'Where are you going?' His English was polished, not forced. With an authentic cheerfulness, unmistakably Desmond.

'Our bus broke down back there so we're walking to the next village. Do you know how much further it is?' The man looked at both of us in turn.

'Oh, it is quite far. You should go back,' he said nodding in the direction we'd come from. Karina held the back of my arm.

'But do you know how far the next village is?' she said. 'Could we get there by nightfall?'

'You should go back to your bus,' the man said again. There was an earnestness about him which was strangely soothing.

'He's right, you know,' I said quietly to Karina, who was already nodding. 'We have no idea how far it is or even whether anything's there.' I suddenly felt quite foolish.

'Thank you,' I said to the man. 'We'll gladly take your advice.' I took Karina's hand and turned around.

'God bless you,' he said as we started walking back.

'How strange,' I said to Karina when we were out of earshot. 'What's he doing out here all on his own?' I realised I hadn't even bothered to ask.

'I know,' she said. 'And such a nice man. It was impossible to argue.'

As she said the words I had a sudden urge to look back. I squeezed her hand and she stopped.

'Where the hell did he go?'

'What do you mean?' We both turned and stood staring at the empty space in front of the tree. He was nowhere to be seen and the tree wasn't nearly wide enough for him to hide behind. I wanted to run back and look, but a sudden breeze whisked dust across the road and rustled the leaves of the tree.

'I think we've just seen an angel,' I whispered. We stood in silence, staring at the vacant shadow. It felt strangely comforting. Karina's eyes glistened in the orange glow of the setting sun. With her dusty face and grubby t-shirt she looked more beautiful than I could ever recall.

A v-formation of birds flew overhead in the direction of the bus, as if showing us the way back. 'Come on, let's get going. It'll be dark soon.'

Walking back I felt so light on my feet I could have run all the way. It was only then I began to take in the magnitude of what had just happened. I didn't consciously shake my head as I looked up. To know and appreciate there is a higher power looking out for you is immensely humbling. For a while we walked in our own grateful silence.

Gradually in the creeping dusk we made out the shape of our stranded bus. By the time we got there, tall flames licked the darkness in a euphoric dance. Everyone was gathered around the fire, so we sat down a few feet away and leant against our packs.

Those passengers closest waved for us to join them, shuffling along to make space. They seemed more excited still that we'd returned. One of the men approached the fire and scraped away two green bananas from the coals to let them cool, then walked over and handed them to us. A few of the others were already eating.

'Thank you,' I nodded and peeled away the skin and took a bite. It tasted just like potato. When we'd finished they brought us another. Then a tin mug of water. We shared it gratefully.

With night folding round us we sat until the flames turned to embers. People had started climbing back into the bus for warmth. So we unrolled our sleeping bags and lay staring at the Milky Way stretching across the sky, all pastel and pearl. The stars glistened in rhythm with the crickets, like a steady heartbeat.

Then, unmistakably, came the sound of a hymn. Except for two young boys still poking the coals, everyone had taken up their places on the bus, their silhouettes etched against steamy windows.

'Tell me you can hear that,' I said.

'Sure can,' Karina said, squeezing my hand a little tighter.

It started softly, then a few more joined in. The men a low, steady drone, the women a soulful soprano, all in perfect harmony. The hymns I knew well, but the words were in Swahili. It was God's music, under God's perfect sky.

'And just when I thought this night couldn't get more magical,' Karina said.

'I love you,' was all I could muster. I closed my eyes, sending teardrops down my temples. And on that night, under those stars, holding the hand of that woman, my heart swelled and burst, its blood flowing freely into Africa's thirsty soil.

oOo

I have often reflected on that day, seeing God's Desmond. It's still the only time I've experienced God in physical form and the brightest-yet sign-post of my faith.

But there have been other occasions, too, when I have undoubtedly known God's presence. Years later in a shared house in London's Willesden Green, I was at one of the lower points in my life, in a wrangling break up, feeling down and with a general sense of displacement in the world. Lying on my bed, staring up at the ceiling I asked God earnestly for help. I needed a sign to know He was there.

It started as a quickened pulse, then being bathed in soothing warmth, a tingling light permeating through my body. The pulse grew stronger, opening my heart from the inside as light poured in from above. It kept coming, filling my heart until I felt it might explode. Tears flowed around my ears as I clutched the quilt. All I could say was 'Thank you, God' a thousand times over.

There was such purity in that light, invisible, but as clear as day. It was overwhelmingly peaceful, incomparably beautiful. I lay still for a long time and when I finally got up, I felt both elated and ashamed to have tested my faith, a jaded Judas.

It made me reflect on how we keep asking for signs, as if faith somehow slips through our fingers and we need a refresher. But the wonderful thing is that when we do need it, it comes. We are fallible creatures after all, our memories and feelings fade and we need to experience to believe.

Matthew wrote in 7:7 that if you ask, it will be given to you; if you seek you will find; and if you knock, the door will be opened. That's how it goes.

It would be in Sydney years later when the next experience came, again in the wake of a separation. The relationship had blown me off course, distracting me from my writing and my gut was screaming. After the relationship ended, I got straight back into constructive rhythms, I spent time on inward reflection and doing things that felt right.

It was a quiet Saturday morning and my housemate was away. As I took my plate to the kitchen I had to suddenly stop and put it down, then hold onto the table as I was overwhelmed by a feeling of intense warmth. A beam of light appeared from the ceiling and pierced my frontal lobe, gushing into my mind. It filled my whole body from the top down, with that same basking glow.

Then I heard a voice, as clearly as if it was right beside me. 'Do not fear. You are on the right path. Keep doing what you are doing.'

In that moment I felt complete love, complete joy and complete peace. How long it lasted for I can't say, but it was no fleeting moment. I wanted to hold onto it, not to let it fade. I was so caught up in it I didn't feel any tears that time, I just saw the wet patches on my t-shirt as I stared into the bathroom mirror soon after. God was there behind my searching eyes, I could feel Him. But it would be a long time before I understood that the God I experienced within, was in fact my true self.

oOo

With one of the most advanced welfare systems in the world, it's no wonder Scandinavia is selective about who they let in. And when a 24-year-old South African backpacker came knocking on their door, the reception was as frosty as a winter fjord.

My emigrating was the only hope Karina and I had of being together. I needed a Schengen visa every time I visited and each lasted only for the duration of my stay. And when you keep going back to the same place, the next application just gets harder.

Our hearts couldn't take seeing each other just four or five times a year, who knew for how long and she wasn't about to give up her state-funded medical degree. We'd talked about marriage, but being so early in our lives and after just a year of back-and-forth, we both knew it would be foolhardy. So there was never going to be a happy ending to our story.

I remember the phone call well. It was not even six weeks since she'd returned home from Cape Town, the adoration and love of my family tucked away neatly in the folds of her Harare Central Hospital doctor's coat.

There was a seminal moment when we both knew but neither of us could say it. All avenues had been exhausted, we'd reached the end of our long and dusty road.

When the receiver clicked into place, I dropped to the ground and sat staring at the emptiness. It seeped slowly into my pores and filled my veins, then wrapped around my heart and squeezed. And squeezed.

I wailed deeply, the kind where no sound comes out. I slid sideways down the wall until my head rested on the floor. If I could have gone further, I would have. Then I watched the tears form a little pool on top of my nose. I wanted to vanish.

There was no mercy that day, or for some while yet. When time is your only friend, it can cruelly slow its course. I kept searching my deserted beaches for her footprints.

It was years before I was capable of loving again and I've never found a love like it since. It changed me, because once you've known such a love, it's hard to find peace until you have it again. Eventually I grew tired of chasing the same shadows and realised I was better off alone. It was just easier that way.

I also realised one of life's greatest ironies, that we fear being alone above all else, yet it's the time we get to learn the most about ourselves. It's an essential part of our make-up.

Even within the most nurturing relationships we need time to be alone, to self-reflect. To self-admonish and self-admire, to find self-love. I know now that it's only in this way that we can sustain wholesome and lasting bonds with each another. It's the only way we can expect to be the best versions of ourselves and to reach our full potential.

I have found love more than once since Karina, each relationship special in its own way. And after each one I have made time to be alone, so I can learn more about myself and cherish all that was good. Each has been an important part of my journey, part of what makes me who I am today, simple cause and effect.

I often wonder whether those that never find love, I mean really find it, might be better off. If you never know it, you never crave it. And if you never lose it, you never have to know that kind of hurt.

I asked Cathy once if she regretted never having a man in her life. She looked at me quizzically and said 'Matthew, I have a man in my life every day. I am married to Jesus.' That has always stuck with me, but it is only all these years later, as I have come to know God in my own way that I have understood.

I know I will find enduring romantic love, or rather that it will find me and in that I am content. The most beautiful thing, though, is understanding that love is around us all the time. It is, after all, the very essence of our being, the very reason those of us that have the least are often the most fulfilled. Undoubtedly the happiest people I have come across are those from the poorest countries in my travels, Malawi, Cambodia, Indonesia. They have themselves, they have one another and they have God. Just in their own individual wrappers.

It is in knowing this that the curse of the developed world has become so clear to me. How we grow up being force-fed that happiness comes from what's around us, what we have, where we live, how we compare to our neighbour. We crave validation to feed our egos and the more we feed the beast, the harder it is to tame.

The secret to happiness isn't taught in any textbook. It lies within the scriptures, yes, but I could only decipher them when I had the code that lay within. It waited there patiently for me and it was only when I awakened to it that my journey to happiness could begin. Life started again, except there was no limit to what I could achieve. All I needed to do was believe.

There are many things Karina taught me in that short year we were together. Perhaps the product of South Africa's traditional ways, but as a man I saw myself as her natural protector. I felt a responsibility to guide and nurture her.

Mum was one of the brightest students in her class yet was denied the opportunity to go to university, something she desperately craved. In the eyes of her parents, home-making was a far more honourable occupation. She spent years of her precious youth waiting for letters and phone calls and willingly dedicated her life to God and Dad's ministry.

Thankfully we've progressed much as a western society, but rightly or wrongly, growing up with those influences left a mark on me. And it was only in being with a woman of Karina's sway and stature that I could understand the true meaning of equality.

Caught in that horde of desperate poverty at Mbeya bus station, I was unashamedly afraid. For Karina of course, as her perceived shepherd I needed to keep her from harm, but for myself also. Yet in the face of such adversity she didn't falter.

Above all else I admired her tenacity and purity of spirit. It was never my help she needed, just my companionship and my love in return. I can safely say I gave her both in abundance. Perhaps it's why we were so good together.

7
London calling

After leaving Karina in Queensland on that first encounter, Richard and I headed across the Tasman to New Zealand where we bagged some much-needed under the table work. Then with coffers replenished, we hitchhiked around both islands. It's those times when you rely on the generosity of others that you really appreciate our connectedness as humans. Strangers going out of their way to take us where we wanted to go, or somewhere better. Putting us up for the night or putting us in touch with other strangers down the road.

We saw the country in a way we could never have on our own, all the while sampling an abundance of home-grown Kiwi hospitality. We went whichever way the wind blew, with ample time to take it all in.

It was a providence that followed us to the US mainland after a stop in Hawaii for the Pipe Masters surf contest. In California we met up with a close school friend who'd flown over to meet us for part of our travels. First stop was downtown LA where we cruised Long Beach Boulevard in his cousin Peter's 1965

Fleetwood Cadillac convertible to the mesmeric beat of local band Sublime.

Boarding the plane back to South Africa three months later, Sean was glad to be alive but felt robbed of a much-anticipated tour of the southern US states. We'd picked up a palm-green Honda Civic for US$500, then driven over 4 000 kilometres down the Mexican coast to a tourist town called Peurto Vallarta. And when we limped back across the Arizona border two-and-a-half months later, I couldn't help but look up into the clear desert sky and give God a little high five.

The idea that three surfer boys sleeping rough in a sedan wasn't going to attract the attention of every Mexican authority was, in hindsight, laughable. Paying the bribes just wasn't in our budget. And losing our passports and immigration papers on a tequila binge was an own-goal we could frankly have done without. It meant several round trips to Guadalajara five hours away and enlisting the help of anxious parents. Besides further denting our coffers, it also meant a truncated tour of the Grand Canyon, Joshua Tree National Park and Las Vegas on our eventual loop back to LA.

We sold the banged-up Civic for US$450 but two months later it was found abandoned on Route 66 with a blown engine, nothing but bad karma in the boot. From there it was on to Washington State, Vancouver, Calgary, Colorado, Florida, Pennsylvania and New York. We crashed with friends we'd met on our travels, hitchhiked the Canadian Rockies, made new friends on flights who took us in and missed some nights entirely courtesy of downtown Miami parties as we were re-acquainted with old girlfriends. It meant that in four-and-a-half months travelling North America we didn't spend a single dime on resting our heads. We lived on the charity of others, not sought but offered, often by complete strangers.

So on the final flight to London a year after leaving home and with no more than loose change in our back pockets, I couldn't help thinking there was more to it than chance. That there was some mysterious force at work. There were just too many close calls, too many M-16 assault rifles pointed in our direction, too many tense negotiations with police in broken English, for us to have walked away unscathed. Mum and Dad could finally down tools and I offered a quiet little prayer of my own. To them and to God. The engine room had been working on overdrive for long enough.

In the bustle of Heathrow, I spotted a South African flag embroidered on a lone traveller's backpack, so I walked over to introduce myself. His cold apathy was somewhat surprising, but I realised we were now on a path more well-trodden. It was July 1998 and the post-apartheid floodgates were wide open. The anonymity of being back in the herd was both strangely jarring and comforting, jarring because we'd lost our draw card, but comforting because we'd no longer be branded racist.

As friendly and welcoming as we'd found people to be, many simply couldn't reconcile the fact we were white and from Africa. Others couldn't see past our role as the oppressor, both to good and bad effect. It stung and no amount of cajoling would sway their views.

It also made me feel ashamed of the stigma that we'd earned as a nation, even to the uneducated. I wondered what it would take for Nelson Mandela's legacy to reach their shores, for our nation to heal in the eyes of others. Perhaps it was just too convenient to keep it that way and as we disappeared into the bowels of London's Underground, I couldn't help choke back a pang of remorse.

Richard was born in Cambridge when Mum and Dad lived there for a two-year stint early in Dad's ministry, before District Six. With a British passport, work was easy to find, while I had to grovel for underpaid hospitality gigs.

London can be brutally cold and unwelcoming, but we found instant solace in the arms of its blossoming club scene. On the dance floors and after-parties of the city's busiest venues we forged friendships that would make London home for the next 12 years and weave the social fabric for our adult lives.

Once settled though, we enjoyed long weekends on the ski fields of Austria, France and Switzerland complements of the pioneering low-cost airlines. When I wasn't seeing Karina, we holidayed in South-East Asia, North Africa and the Med. And after two years of a carefree, hazy existence with a newly-broken heart, it was time to head home and get serious about a career.

It was a new millennium and the dreaded Y2K passed without so much as a fizzle so I set about looking for a job. South Africa was in the vice-like grip of affirmative action after the change in government and as a white male I had hardly been disadvantaged. Setting aside my first-class education, it would now be the colour of my skin that saw job applications head to the bottom of the pile. So with a four-year ancestral visa for the UK compliments of Grandmother Doris, I headed back to London to find my fortune.

Besides its grey and dreary façade, the city had captured my heart with its kaleidoscope of people and unpretentious nature. It was only on leaving Cape Town that I realised how truly small it was. For all its natural beauty it was stiflingly cliquey. In this sprawling new metropolis I found a place where I could just be, no expectations and no judgement.

But if I was going to succeed, I needed to pick up the pace. People in the square mile walked like they were perpetually late and if you didn't keep up you got run over. I'd have to fight my way in, be prepared to roll up my sleeves and get dirty. But once I did, I soon realised that underneath the city's grimy streets ran rivers of gold.

The London with money and the London without are entirely different places, like opposites sides of the Berlin wall. Once you find the rub of the green it's a wonderland, a smorgasbord of culture, history, theatre and circus. It grows on you like ivy up a church spire. And with each of Big Ben's chimes its heartbeat got louder and louder until one day I found myself helplessly in love.

Getting on the ladder though, was another matter.

In the early 2000s the internet was in its infancy and Google wasn't a word yet. So I found an article in PR Week magazine featuring the 50 fastest-growing consultancies. I wrote to all of them. A couple of botched interviews later I found myself staring at the name 'College Hill Associates' embossed in marble behind a knock-out receptionist. It was the final of only three responses and the only firm appearing vaguely corporate. It felt like my speed and perhaps I'd get to use my hard-earned degree after all. My palms were sweaty.

Four interview rounds later it was my South African roots that landed me the gig, the irony not lost on me. With apartheid sanctions a thing of the past, the firm had made a name advising many of its corporate behemoths as they looked to expand offshore. It seemed that I'd lend a sprig of authenticity to their British pomp.

With the two countries' historic ties, London was the natural port of call for raising capital and I was the guy who would help sell their dream. Green as a gooseberry at first, I slowly clawed my way in, more by grit that grace. But they saw enough potential to take a punt and I made sure to repay their faith. Six years later I was their youngest ever partner.

At first encounter the excitement of the corporate world is surpassed only by the allure of money. That powerful intangible force that makes our world go round ... the more rats on the wheel, the faster it goes. You could almost smell it on your fingers.

It's easy to get caught up in the bright lights. Rubbing shoulders with the c-suite over Michelin star dinners, buzzing on adrenaline-fuelled all-nighters and swilling champagne as if it were mineral water. And all with someone else's money.

First it consumes you, then it defines you. You drive a nice car, wear fitted Italian suits and buy a bachelor pad. But you're only as good as the next pay rise. Then one day you find you're going on holiday just to tell people where you've been and it all seems perfectly normal.

The highs and lows of the dotcom bubble, 9/11 and global financial crisis were all as tragically unpredictable as they were severe, hitching a ride on the rollercoaster of hope and praying you didn't fall out. There was an edginess to it all, an urgency that paid no heed to what was right or wrong. As long as it made money, everyone was happy. But were they really? At the end of the day, it was all about ego and there's only so much dick-swinging one can take.

How many corporate lifers slip on the gold Rolex and retreat through the revolving door of oblivion, washing down their sense of purpose with each less satisfying Pina Colada? Or suddenly succumb to heart failure or cancer? It was easily done because it was all they knew. Their job was their identity yet how effortlessly they got replaced.

I wonder how much of that comes down to fear. Fear of the unknown, of when they'll next be needed or wanted and maybe not at home. Fear of not knowing how to think about themselves without the shiny suit. How many times did they stare into the country club mirror and wonder who they were looking at? Another Scotch please.

Buddha said 'It's okay to lose people. But never lose yourself.' I was too young and naïve to understand this when I started corporate life. I was on the journey of self-admiration, of fattening my ego, of finding financial freedom so I didn't have to suffer the same hardship Mum and Dad did.

I'd spent my life as a fish out of water – the English kid in Afrikaner country, the white boy in coloured communities, the penniless minister's son in a world of private school privilege. I'd rebelled against it without even realising what it was. Now I'd finally found my own sense of identity, of self-worth and I revelled in it. Life was grand.

But it never felt natural. It was gritty, even, like a grain of sand in the eye that just wouldn't flush. And it would take a different hand-me-down from Mum and Dad to set me straight and ultimately open the doorway of my spiritual journey.

oOo

Anxiety is a millstone inherited from both sides of the family, especially Mum's. Both Mum and my sisters have worked hard to keep Grandmother Dulcie's neurosis at bay, with commendable success. There's no cure so we've all learned to live with it. But circumstance can be a great aggravator and what started as an annoyance through high school and university grew to plague my career and ultimately reach debilitating levels.

It was 4 pm on the day we'd reported our financial results to the market. I was head of media relations for the FTSE100 financial services company Old Mutual and I had done an all-nighter to finalise the materials, then supported the CEO in delivering some tricky messaging. The day itself had gone well enough, but I'd all but tuned out by the time he faced the lectern for our town hall meeting. My eyes bleeding from fatigue, I was contemplating that first deliciously cold beer when he unexpectedly called me up to address the company on our media programme.

Jolted like when the bungee cord catches, I was wrenched from my daydream and thrown centre stage, three hundred pairs of expectant eyes boring into my skull like miniature jackhammers. It's at moments like these you expect your years of PR training to kick in, flipping straight to autopilot and navigating a smooth descent. But that's the tricky thing about anxiety. It's exactly at these moments when experience counts for nought. There's a veil that comes down and envelopes your whole body, like a silent force field shutting down all known senses and instinct. And a heat that builds from the depths of your core until you think you might spontaneously combust. What happens next is anyone's guess. You just pray you packed your parachute.

I opened my mouth and words came out. In a haze the throng of bodies changed shape as if a distant mirage. More words, even some laughter. There was a glimmer of hope they were sensible. Was I going to make it through after all? No. I was mid-flow when my CEO, direct boss and ultimate lifeline to the firm strode back to the lectern and cut me short. When I turned to look at my seat in the front row it was like looking the wrong way through binoculars. Perhaps the floor would graciously swallow me along the way. No again.

The worst part about anxiety is that you lose all perception. There's an all-consuming self-deprivation that follows in its wake that has no patience for rationality. Like lava flowing through a forest, it obliterates everything in its path, leaving no traces that might help to soothe your perspective. The good bits just don't count and what's left of you then suffocates in its toxic fumes. The only thing that helps is eventual sleep, but even that has to end.

In isolation these events are surmountable, but they're never isolated. Each experience becomes more excruciating than the one before. Then it creeps into your daily life. You begin clamming up at smaller group meetings, then conference calls. Even a confrontation in the supermarket or getting a dressing down from your partner ... the seeds of uncertainty permeate your being until you can no longer face yourself in the mirror. You just can't see the wood for the trees. Your only options are to face it head on or run away and once again I chose the latter.

Having seen a major financial services company through the global financial crisis as well as some of its own making, it was time to pull the pin. I'd also fallen for a vivacious German lady named Nina. From the very first date she'd talked about going travelling and while I'd been buying time, the pressure was mounting.

Meanwhile, life in London had reached a natural crossroads. One of my best friends with whom I owned a house in West Acton got married and was moving out. My sisters had been living with us on their own London adventures, but were both moving on. And the saturating, soggy cold of London had finally reached my bones. It was time for change, for some sunshine, for my mistress Australia.

Once more I packed my life into a backpack and hit the road, this time with my lover not my brother. With a bulging bank account it was a different experience entirely, one that kicked off with the 2010 Football World Cup in South Africa after a month in my beloved Malawi. Like Australia, it had made such a mark the first time that I'd vowed to return.

In no time I was re-acquainted with its beautiful people, shedding any remnants of materialism. It reminded me of who I really was, like backpacking in my birthday suit. Nina and I took soccer balls and pencils for the children, we made pen pals at the Livingstone orphanage, feasted on fresh goat for a village chief's birthday and recharged our batteries of humanity beside its enchanting lake. It was the perfect anaesthetic, the frayed edges of London soon a long distant memory.

It would be the start of a new adventure that saw us land on Australian shores some 15 months later, including six months each in South America and South East Asia. Our richest experiences were once again in their poorest countries. Persecuted not a generation ago by the Khmer Rouge, Cambodian people are some of the most gracious and generous humans on earth and while still reeling from the tsunami that wiped out entire bloodlines, Indonesia remained a beautiful melting pot of culture and kindness. Their resilience of spirit in the face of such adversity was as eye opening as it was humbling. It came to personify everything we had so conveniently forgotten.

But it would be in Thailand where I would have an experience so profound that it changed the course of my life. Were it not for the ladies of the 10 Baht Bar I would not have written these pages and wherever the women are, I will always be in their debt.

8
Human traffic

Nina and I disembarked at Kanchanaburi station, a sleepy town in the north-west of Thailand famed in the 1957 film *The Bridge on the River Kwai*. The movie depicted the construction of a 415-kilometre railway between Thailand and Burma during the Second World War, dubbed Death Railway after the 13 000 prisoners of war and nearly 100 000 civilians that lost their lives at the hands of the Japanese while building it. Their bodies are still buried along its now discarded tracks.

It was the first leg of our Southeast Asia trip and Nina's friend Simona had joined us from Munich. We were excited to visit one of Thailand's more preserved regions, tucked away from the tired backpacker trails that have scarred its treasured culture.

What we didn't know about Kanchanaburi though was the murky colour of its underbelly. Beyond the glaring eye of mainstream tourism, along its myriad bars, cane barstools propped up pale-fleshed, prowling westerners like a line-up of clown heads at a carnival. It was the perfect place to disappear, where the whisky was as cheap as the girls were young. Where they could feel like men, thousands of miles from anyone who would have them do so willingly.

Aarya was 21 when we met her that first night in the 10 Baht Bar. Open to the street, its bright neon lights and cheesy 90s beats lured in passers-by for a sweet mojito or SangSom bucket. The three of us were ushered in by a bevy of lively hostesses who couldn't get enough of our stories of wild travels and our strange accents. As the night wore on, we played pool, drinking shots from neon plastic glasses and cramming into selfies under a disco of whirling insects.

Aarya's English was distinctly more refined, complements of a colonial Burmese education. Dark mocha skin lent an exotic flair to her natural beauty, her eyes lively as the drink, yet tempered before her time.

Of all the girls, she was the most curious about the places we'd been, the people we'd met, the stories we'd earned. In return we learned of her proficiency with languages, her approaching degree in engineering and her two younger siblings at home in Mandalay. There were shades of brightness about her which were captivating, yet overshadowed at times by an awkward wariness, as if she kept remembering. We would soon learn why.

Come the witching hour, we watched in horror as a thick-set female proprietor tapped them on the shoulder in turn. Each would disappear to the back room to freshen her lipstick and brush her hair, then re-emerge to perch next to an overweight, tattoo-riddled predator nursing a perspiring lager.

The men for their part avoided our stares, perhaps too ashamed or just too busy ogling. And before the booze-fuelled anger could take over, I grabbed Nina and Simona by the hands and slunk away into the humid night.

Nina would be the undeserving recipient of my anger that night, as much as I was of hers, like we'd both been thrown into someone else's ring. It was necessary madness, but under a creaking ceiling fan the solace of sleep defied me that night. Nothing would blur the images burning in my mind's eye, no food or drink quell the creeping nausea.

As a new day broke over the Kwai, I stood staring out of our floating bamboo hut at the pond skaters going about their business, admiring the freedom with which they glided across the undisturbed glass-like surface.

Nina came up from behind and wrapped her arms around me, breaking my thoughts. 'Couldn't sleep either, huh?' I just pulled her in closer.

'Last night …' I said eventually.

'I know. Me too.'

'I can't get it out of my head.'

For a while we stood in silent embrace. I had nothing but deep empathy for Nina, for how she might feel being a woman. I pictured Aarya waking in another strange bed, wondered what she might have dreamed and whether she had any place she might call home.

We returned to the 10 Baht Bar that night, apprehensive but with our eyes wide open. I needed to speak to Aarya, to understand how and why. Or perhaps just to quell my own unease.

The same smiling girls greeted us, only this time like long-lost friends. In and among the frivolity we knew to be their only elixir, we managed to snatch Aarya away for a spell. Had she worn the pain of her story you wouldn't have known it:

She'd been sold to Burmese traffickers by her own parents. They had no other option, the money she made put food on their table, she said. It meant her brother and sister could go to school, maybe one day to university. It had given them a chance of a better life.

Poverty can be a cruel master and her own hourglass had run out of sand. Seeing her family only in her dreams, they were happy, thriving even, she said. It was all that allowed her to sleep at night under sweat-stained sheets.

It was a common trade, scooping up beautiful young girls and marching them along Death Railway under the veil of a new moon, straight into the arms of servitude. How many of her pennies would trickle back along its broken tracks, I wondered? How many nights crushed under lecherous monsters, choking on their panting, acrid breath. They might just as well have laid a fresh grave and written her name in the sand.

Aarya had no idea how long she would be there. The girls were her family now she said and she was theirs. She needed to be strong for them, they looked up to her, followed her example. Each of them wrote home frequently but all that came back was cool assurance from their oppressors. It was a life built on trust and hope.

Come midnight and the same song played on the juke box. Different men this time but wearing the same uniform. We didn't hang around for it, just exchanged details and bid our farewells. And as our sleeper train bound for Chiang Mai clattered across the River Kwai the next afternoon, it wasn't the souls of those who died building it that occupied my mind.

I wondered how far I might have to go along the meandering shore before I'd stumble across a father crouched at its edge, staring into the swirling tea-coloured water as he mourned the loss of his first born. If her brother and sister might study a little harder knowing of her sacrifice, or whether the guilt would forever cloud their own journeys. The cruel injustice of it all was impossible to reconcile.

A spluttering air conditioner snapped me back to the carriage. I stared up at a piece of tickertape flapping in the burst of cold air. Such a luxury Aarya would surely only know in the arms of her next perpetrator. I slunk back against the faux leather seat and watched the sun droop through a milky haze. I felt powerless and raw.

Zopiclone alone would get me through the 16-hour journey north that followed. But that time in Kanchanaburi kept tapping away at my conscience like a vivid, recurring dream. From the corner of my eye, I'd see Aarya disappear around a Chiang Mai street corner, or a flash of her yellow singlet at the far end of the food markets. A song we'd danced to would drift out from a nearby bar, like I wasn't allowed to forget.

It stirred in me an unshakeable yearning to act and it is Aarya who ultimately led me to take up writing. It was the only channel I knew to try and make a difference, perhaps by just a few more people being aware of the plight of so many caught in the web of global trafficking. Or stoking up enough public ire that the offenders might think twice before boarding the next plane. But stand idly by as they gorged on the cadavers of tomorrow's Aaryas I simply could not.

With every passing day the yearning grew and once settled in Sydney a novel depicting Aarya as its female protagonist began to take shape. It would be the birth of a pastime that has seen me find my true passion and while the pages on which she still rests have been set aside for now, my hope is one day to finish her story.

9
No spare room for denial

Wrapping up our travels with a week on my favourite Indonesian surf beach, Balangan, I could not have been further removed from the strain of corporate life. And it was only once Nina and I were nestled in with my sister in a small two-bedroomed apartment in Sydney's seaside suburb of Dee Why that the anxiety returned in earnest.

Our arrival in Sydney wasn't exactly met with the tickertape parade my CV might have warranted. Granted, being on a travel visa, an employer would need to sponsor me, but the magnificent beaches and weather felt a deceptive façade to Australia's parochial ways, while in the wake of the global financial crisis the market barely had a pulse.

Ten months into a fruitless search, therefore, and on the verge of buying tickets back to Europe, a proprietor of a small PR agency offered me a job that I snapped up like an enthusiastic Audrey in the Little Shop of Horrors. I was in no mood to throw in the towel of my Australian dream.

What surprised me, though, was how uninspiring the work was. Perhaps it was the environment, perhaps the fact that my heart was still on a beach somewhere in the Pacific. But I struggled to get motivated and soon I felt the grip of anxiety tightening.

Another problem was that Nina was not exactly enamoured with Australia. She'd gone from filing breaking geopolitical stories at Associated Press in London, to shovelling trivia down the throats of bogan Australia on Channel 10. The nausea of competing with high-heeled fake tan millennials, compounded by nearly a year of supporting us on her meagre wage had pushed her, and us, to breaking point.

I thought that finally bringing in money would help. We'd agreed not to make any rash decisions and moving into our own place would ultimately be the test. But it was just window dressing and seven months in, a heavy air of inevitability awaited me as I turned the key to our new Darlington apartment. There was no spare room for denial.

The break-up was brutal. Four years is a lot of emotional and psychological investment for no reward, at least that's what it felt like at the time. The stress of moving out and finding my feet again was all consuming and even as I packed my Jeep and headed to Manly, the pristine gateway to Sydney's Northern Beaches, dark clouds of despair kept gathering overhead. I was overwhelmed by the feeling that something fundamental was missing in my life. I was alarmingly out of sorts, that don't-want-to-get-out-of-bed kind. I needed a shake-up, to plant my feet back on mother earth.

It was a Saturday morning when the email came, just as my train sidled under a graffiti-clad bridge and I thought 'what's the fucking point?' It was from Emma, our English friend we'd met in a beach bar on Palawan Island. After leaving the

Philippines, she and her partner went to India to try different forms of meditation, their own little spiritual Petri dish on the slopes of the Himalayas. By then I had a long-nurtured desire to try meditation but never found the right entry point, so I pleaded with her to share their experience. The email was her reply.

Having been back in the UK for several months she was apologetic for the tardiness, but arriving on that day, on that journey, I could only smile at the coincidence. What's more, the report card couldn't have been clearer. They'd found the perfect practice to suit my life and lifestyle, called Transcendental Meditation. So before the train docked at North Sydney station I had called Sydney's TM centre to make an appointment.

What instantly struck me on the introductory course were the principals on which the practice was founded. A 5 000-year-old Vedic tradition reincarnated in the 1950s by Maharishi Mahesh Yogi, TM is today practised by millions of people around the world. Maharishi's vision was to bring about world peace, not by everyone loving one another, but by first loving themselves. Because it is only by loving ourselves that we can truly love one another. It was such a simple premise, yet so profound.

I quickly set into a blissful rhythm, 20 minutes in the morning before work, then another 20 minutes when I got home. The first set me up for the working day, the second switched me off from it, reconnecting me with the present.

Its true elegance lay in its simplicity. By focusing on a personal mantra I could avoid all thought, until slowly the mantra, too, drifted away and I transcended into an altered state of awareness. Described as the unity state or fourth state of consciousness, unlike being awake, asleep or dreaming, I was aware of what was happening around me, while being immersed in a state of complete euphoria.

I started sleeping well, no more tossing to the ticking clock on a Sunday night. I began to feel more grounded, like I was an inch taller yet walking two feet closer to the earth. I felt entirely more balanced, more patient, more at peace.

Gradually, the fog began to lift. I could think more clearly, my decisions were sharper. I felt more energised, more attuned to what my body wanted and needed. I started paying more attention to cravings and desires. If I felt tired I rested and if I felt the urge for pasta, I ate pasta. It was like the communication channels between my body and mind had been cleared out and new wiring put in.

But these were just the physical benefits. They were easy to understand and acknowledge. I had never felt better and if that had been the extent of it I would still have believed I'd discovered the world's best kept secret for a long and trouble-free life.

But it was just the beginning, like planting a seed without knowing what will grow, then one day finding yourself at the top of a giant beanstalk peeking through the clouds of human perception, into a world of unbounded possibility. It was the non-physical attributes that would alter my course of understanding of all that we are and of our purpose as humanity. These things came much more gradually.

Eight months in I did the first of TM's advanced techniques, practised just before bed so you gain all the benefits of meditation while sleeping. My instructor was a Vedic expert from India, a gentle man with a benevolent smile called Mr Jenna. He was a few inches shorter than me, yet sitting beside him I was dwarfed by his presence. Before we began, he asked me a few questions, like when I had started practising, whether it was regular, what my experience had been. Then he paused. 'And have you noticed anything different in your life?' he asked. I looked at him curiously. His expression was one of suggestion, not inquisition, a seeking smile in the waiting room.

'Do you mean, have I noticed things becoming easier, more aligned?' I asked. He simply cocked his head to one side and nodded. 'Yes. Actually, now that you mention it, I really have.'

'Good. Let us begin.'

It was in that moment that everything made sense, like the scales had fallen from my eyes. Everything I'd noticed had been falling into place with beautiful synchronicity, like seamless transport connections, social conflicts getting naturally resolved, even clients shifting impossible deadlines. When I thought of these things in isolation they meant nothing, perhaps some good fortune. But I realised then there was something much more complex at play.

Today I always notice these instances and with each passing year they grow more frequent. They are constant reminders of the beautiful unification of our existence.

Abraham Hicks, a spiritual entity described as 'a group consciousness from the non-physical dimension' channelled through Esther Hicks, teaches us about the Law of Attraction. That what we offer vibrationally is the path of least resistance. It's the art of letting things happen naturally, of creating our own pathways through thoughts and intentions. The less we resist the more we live in flow; every roaring river starts as a trickle down a riverbed.

It is through my meditation practice that I connect to my inner source of energy, the unified field that flows within each of us and forms the very fabric of all existence. Each time I come out, I bring some of it with me so that day by day, month by month, year by year my connection with self has grown and become a more natural part of who I am, all of the time. It was in that moment, sitting in the chair besides the diminutive Mr Jenna that my awakening began.

Ever since communicating with Mike in the afterlife I've pondered what could be possible. And it is through meditation that I began to wonder what we are capable of by harnessing the power of the mind. Or more to the point, what is beyond the mind.

The seed was planted in my teens, again by Sean's parents. Besides being a medium, Debbie and her husband David regularly practised a form of meditation learned from Native American Indians. They spoke of travels to different worlds and encounters with other life forms. When you're the son of an Anglican priest, it's a pretty hard pill to swallow, but these were salt-of-the-earth people who I trusted with my life. It blew my troubled teenage mind.

> **Epiphany** – *'a sudden and surprising moment of understanding'*

It was January 2019 and I was driving up a winding tree-lined road to Sydney Conference & Training Centre to join 80 fellow meditators for a retreat. The twelfth of January was Maharishi's birthday and bears great significance in the TM calendar. Before his death, each year he would reappear from a week-long silent retreat to share his teachings and set new goals for the year. So we were joined by practice leaders from around the world, the energy emanating from our Narrabeen bushland setting quite palpable.

Much of the programme saw us confined to our rooms to repeat sequences of Ayurveda yoga, pranayama and meditation. Walking out on the Sunday afternoon, therefore, I felt robbed. Having had a taster of the enhanced power of even small group sessions, I'd been excited by the prospect of mass meditations. And it wasn't until the wave of euphoria arrived two days later that I realised physical barriers were no impediment to this collective power and that consciousness knows no boundaries.

For the next three days I floated around like my gravity had been unplugged. It was one still morning while meditating upstairs in my Manly townhouse that I experienced a connection with source energy for the first time. Quite rhythmically, the divide between the physical and non-physical world disappeared, as if every particle and cell in my body had merged with the air I was breathing. For a time, which could have been minutes or days, I was at one with the cosmos. It was profoundly peaceful and beautiful, like knowing love in its purest form. Like going home.

I was still basking in the glow that evening when the epiphany came, or rather was handed to me as if etched in stone tablets on Mount Sinai. Something our TM teacher had said that weekend stuck with me. She talked of the unified source of energy we tap into each time we transcend as being God, implying that they were one and the same. It was such a simple premise, yet I could never realise it until I felt it for myself.

It was in that moment that I knew without question. As I marvelled at the streaks of pink cloud through my upstairs skylight, I understood for the first time my father's life-long dedication to the Church. I finally understood his calling all those years before, his unquestioning desire to serve God. The one God, the God of love. The Holy Spirit, omnipotent, ever present. Us in Him and He in us.

And it was in that moment that I finally understood the scriptures. All the pieces of the puzzle fell simultaneously into place, the lines disappearing to form a perfectly clear picture.

Christian literature would have us visualise God in human form, so that's how we perceive Him. We're simple creatures, who need to see to believe. But I knew then God to be no more human than our universe is finite. That He is creation, the one source of all truth. The physical and the non-physical, in beautiful harmony.

As the last wisps of pink made way for the brilliant evening star, I wept tears of unbounded joy. The shackles of forty-four years seeking my own truth shattered and fell to the floor. I felt their physical weight lift from my shoulders and I could have flown through that skylight to the stars, for this was surely the greatest moment of my life. To finally know, both in head and heart. It was my own modern-day gospel.

The elation I felt that day was overwhelming. I wanted the whole world to know such a feeling and I finally understood my parents' dedication to sharing their own understanding. To enrich the lives of others by knowing the truth and the sacrifices they were willing to make along the way.

I understood that despite the hardships that came with such a life of servitude, it carried with it no burden. It was their calling, as much as in that moment I understood it to be mine. It may have come late, but the trumpets of Jerusalem sounded and the drums beat, for this was the day that the Lord had come.

Part II

THE GOSPEL

10
The model, the military man and the monk

Life is a rich tapestry of moments woven into a picture of who we are. Most we don't remember but some we can't forget. Within these moments it's the people we spend time with that have the biggest influence on our perspective and perspective is everything. Yet when we distil it, there are only a handful of people that really make a difference to who we become.

Often it's family or a lifelong friend. Sometimes it's a lost friend, or a fleeting acquaintance. They come into our lives for a reason, at exactly the time they're supposed to. We can't change it or chivvy it on. All we can do is be patient and when they do come appreciate them for who they are and what they are there to give us.

Victoria Mills, Charl du Toit and Jude-Martin Etuka are three such people: the model, the military man and the monk. Along my spiritual path they have been shining beacons, uniquely inspiring yet undivided in their beauty as humans.

It was Victoria who guided me here. Through her hardwired connection to God, she has shepherded me away from Aarya's pages to tell my own story. Over countless cups of tea in her magnetic company, I have found my voice and the courage to step into my father's giant shoes.

She is a beacon of hope for anyone lost in the abyss of parental abuse and it was the struggle with her own father that would have her turn her mess into her message. She has been my most influential spiritual guide and mentor and has taught me the real meaning of forgiveness through complete surrender.

From atop a rock in the garden of her Newport home looking over the expanse of Sydney's Northern Beaches, she downloads God's message. It's the culmination of a lifetime of Transcendental Meditation, the only gift from her father she is grateful for and it has inspired her to create a global coaching platform for healing the masses.

Her message is clear and simple. We all have a path chosen for us by God, whatever we believe God to be. But it is only those of us that are truly brave that choose to follow it. We can all make a difference in the world, but we must first choose to make a difference to ourselves. It is Maharishi's same simple roadmap for a peaceful world.

Victoria is by far the most courageous person I know, for finding her way in the darkness that consumed her life for 38 years. For choosing a life of service to humanity when she was denied one of her own. For choosing not to be a victim, but to be *victorious*.

oOo

Like me, Charl du Toit's father, uncle and grandfather were all priests, only we were Anglican while they belonged to the Dutch Reformed Church, which staunchly supported apartheid. It was Prime Minister Daniel François Malan – a former Dutch Reformed minister – that institutionalised apartheid in 1948 and it was under his tutelage that the country's leaders flagrantly propagated its virtues as a birthright of the Afrikaner people.

Charl and I grew up worshipping the same God, just in a different language. We followed different factions of Christianity that taught from the same scriptures, only one embodied love and the other hatred. One recognised all beings as equal in the eyes of God while the other sanctioned slavery. And one led marches in protest against the principles that the other extolled.

We were two men, born of the same era on different sides of white South Africa. The Boer and the Brit. We both had a deep yearning to seek our own answers, to test the doctrines of our faith and faith itself, yet for very different reasons. It is why after hearing his story I was overcome by a deep yearning to share it with the world. And why 18 months later I flew back to South Africa to do just that and get it all down.

Above all else, Charl's story is one of faith in the eyes of absolute adversity. Like Victoria, it would only be through complete surrender that he could come to know God's grace and understand that we are all part of God's plan. And, like Victoria, it is his story that inspired me to be courageous, because had it been me in his shoes, I honestly could not say I would have stayed the course as he did.

But Charl's is also a story of human triumph, of a stubborn refusal to succumb to a doctrine he spent his life being force fed, despite his being broken down time and again by the very people it would have him hate. And it is a story of hope that the country he would have died to protect one day might love him back.

oOo

Jude-Martin Etuka, too, grew up in a deeply religious household. And like my father, he was called to the service of God at a young age. Inspired by the ebullient monks of St Dominic's in Lagos, at just 17 he joined the Dominican Order and took the solemn oath of poverty, chastity and obedience.

The quest of those in the Dominican Order is to come to know and understand God both spiritually and intellectually and it was in Oxford University's Blackfriars Hall that Jude would see out his days as a practising monk.

Alongside his brothers he followed a life of meditation, silence, fasting and assiduous study. While Nigeria's Dominican University had given him rich spiritual fulfilment, it was within the smaller but more keenly-minded Oxford fraternity that Jude would challenge his innate belief system and even the very existence of God.

Both experientially and intellectually he came to know that the path to God is inward. It was by going without that he could journey within and it was by deconstructing and putting back together both Eastern philosophy and Western religion that he would come to understand their beautiful alignment. That we are all seeking a closeness to God, or whatever we choose to call God and that it isn't important how we find God, just that we do.

It is Jude's earned wisdom that has consummated all I have come to realise in my own way. It is through sharing his experience that I have put to bed my doubts and celebrated the marriage of science and mysticism. This has been such a gift, as it has been to spend time with the most enlightened person I know.

11

Charl and his angels

In the middle of South Africa's Eastern Cape bush stands a small house with olive-green walls and an even darker green roof, in stark contrast to its brown and barren surrounds. Thin bands of evergreen gwarrie and schotia trees line the tops of distant hills, a taunting reminder of how the entire valley looked before the five-year drought set in.

A lone electricity pylon casts a long shadow across its dusty, thorn-ridden yard. Through the open kitchen doorway I feel the last of the sun's heat as it slips quickly away, as if ashamed to parch the earth of these good people for yet another day.

Liesl takes the coffee pot from the stove. 'Perhaps it will rain tomorrow,' I say enthusiastically.

'Wouldn't that be nice,' she smiles, drying a cup and placing it on the patterned linoleum table in front of me. 'Not much chance at this time of year.' Her English is remarkably fluent thanks to a post-colonial Zimbabwe education. It's December 2019 and she's contemplating another relentlessly hot and dry Christmas.

She sweeps her dark fringe away from clear blue eyes. Hers is a kind face that does little to portray the hardships that have brought her here, having just re-married for the second time.

Charl stomps up the back steps. He's just visited the outhouse where he does his business, part of an ecological experiment to enrich the soil with the ammonia nitrate. '*Ek kan die koffee nou lekker ruik daar buite,*' as the smell of coffee draws him in from outside.

He swings open the bottom half of the door and gives his wife a peck on the cheek. '*Jy maak altyd die beste koffie,*' complimenting her on the coffee. Then he slides into a wooden chair at the head of the table and he smiles at me. 'Well, the kids are doing a great job planting those avo pips,' he says in his thick Afrikaner accent. 'They'll definitely earn their supper tonight.'

Having rescued a sack of avocados about to turn from the local farm stall bin, Liesl has painstakingly scooped the flesh out of the good ones to freeze and set aside the pips for the vegetable garden. It's all part of their attempt at subsistence living to save money. Each of Liesl's four children have their own small patch, a bit of healthy competition. But with heavily calcified ground and no rain, progress is slow. And with Charl's two kids visiting for the holidays, there are many mouths to feed.

Liesl hands Charl a steaming cup of black coffee and fetches the sugar pot from the tiny pantry. There is no room for kitchen cupboards so everything has its rightful place. '*Dankie, skat,*' he thanks her. His ever lively grey-green eyes peer out from under thick sun-bleached eyebrows, handy for his long days as a game ranger at nearby Schotia Safaris where we met.

A handful of grey strands in his beard are the only evidence of his 49 years. Along with his unkempt hair, it still gleams a natural chestnut colour. There's a beautiful authenticity about him, part of what captivated me on that first meeting. In fact, so favourable was my impression that here I was, two years later, about to have supper with his bourgeoning family.

'So, where do you want to begin?' he beams. It's the perfect way to start any story and his story is the reason I made the journey. Although sitting in that little green house in the middle of God's wilderness I couldn't help feeling we had been brought together by something much more powerful. And after confessing I had no idea where the encounter would take us, he stops me. 'Matt, before we go on, I think we should pray together.'

I smiled back at him. On the long drive up from Cape Town the only message I got was 'pray'. I knew I just had to trust that everything would fall into place the way it should. And even before finishing our first cup of coffee together we were already aligned. I felt completely at ease.

Five minutes later we were standing around the kitchen table holding hands. Me, Liesl, Charl and their six children. It was time to be officially welcomed into their humble home. My heart was about to explode.

Assigned to the scrap heap

Charl du Toit was born in Somerset East on Little Karoo's eastern fringes, a 300- kilometre valley running between the Swartberg and Outeniqua mountain ranges in the country's south. It was his father's first congregation as a minister in the Dutch Reformed Church or NG Kerk and one of many parishes along the Eastern and Western Cape they'd move to before being stationed in Grahamstown as chaplain for the South African Defence Force. It was there that Charl learned to speak English.

On Sundays he would stare up at the ornate pulpit and listen to his father extolling teachings from the 'Great Book'. Unlike many more staunchly conservative leaders of the NG Kerk, his father worked with priests from other denominations – Methodist, Baptist, Lutheran, Presbyterian. So from an early age Charl came to appreciate that these were merely different bottles for the same elixir and that they all worshipped the same almighty God. And while he dutifully studied the scriptures, a practice that remains ingrained in his daily life, he began to question his church's rigid interpretation and to seek his own source of truth.

In 1990 he graduated from Stellenbosch University's Faculty of Military Science and joined the army, mostly out of a sense of duty and honour. Nelson Mandela was about to be released from Robben Island and apartheid was splintering under the strain of global condemnation. Little did he know that when he left the military ten years later, it would be the country he so loved and would have died to defend that would bring about his greatest betrayal.

His forebears were the architects of apartheid and as much as their blood runs in his veins, he laments that apartheid ever existed. But he also laments the brutal atrocities his people suffered under the British, the thousands of Afrikaner women marched off to concentration camps to be systemically raped and abused by soldiers, both black and white. It's not an excuse, but rather an attempt to rationalise his people's course of action.

He regrets the hardships apartheid has inflicted on so many of his fellow countrymen, but also the stigma it has attached to his people. As a white Afrikaner he is automatically labelled racist, an experience I know all too wall from my travels in North America. It can make a man's blood boil.

Three years into Charl's military service, Cape Town was gripped by a wave of terrorism. First the St James Church massacre in Kenilworth, killing 11 white members of the congregation and wounding another 58, then the Heidelberg Massacre in Observatory where another four lost their lives. Both were at the hands of the Azanian People's Liberation Army (APLA), an armed wing of the Pan-Africanist Congress.

The Cape Town bombings were the culmination of a flood of major uprisings across the country as people began to smell apartheid's decay and Charl's platoon was often called into the townships around Grahamstown to support the government's riot control unit, the Afdeling Binnelandse Stabiliteid (ABS). But the protests were mostly peaceful and it was the ABS they had to keep under control not the crowds.

The perpetrators of the APLA attacks would later be granted amnesty under the Truth and Reconciliation Commission, and there were many that couldn't reconcile how no apology was offered. Meanwhile, Charl and his white military comrades watched from the sidelines as their world began to unravel.

He joined the Special Forces but only saw conflict twice due to near-fatal training injuries. After a trench-clearing exercise using live ammunition, some soldiers made a fire with the empty boxes. One of them still contained M26 high-explosive grenades. They went off as the soldiers huddled in to keep warm and Charl escaped with only minor shrapnel wounds, although some of his comrades were far less fortunate.

Then in a night-parachuting incident the wind was so strong that several soldiers were either blown out to sea never to be found or were seriously wounded colliding with walls and fences miles off-course. Charl collapsed his parachute mid-air to descend more quickly and landed so hard he shattered his knee. Had he re-opened it half a second later I wouldn't be writing his story. It was then he suspected God might have other plans for him.

By the late 1990s affirmative action had gripped the military, tighter than any other government institution bar the government itself. While the rank and file were evenly mixed, management and officers were still mostly white and in remedying the situation, cracks began to appear in Special Forces safety standards. But when Charl reported his concerns, he was promptly silenced.

He sombrely speaks of five friends who were killed by their own side. Major Piet van As was shot dead by a 29-year-old platoon commander in the 7 SA Infantry at the Phalaborwa military base in the Northern Province. Van As had given him a poor report card, so he shot his own Company Commander in the back at close range. The culprit later surrendered to the police but was never prosecuted.

In early 2000, Charl was called in to see his black Commanding Officer and told there was no longer any place for whites in the new South Africa. Had he been allowed to stay for another year, he would have received a full military pension and medical aid for his family for life. Instead, they handed him his marching papers and a severance package of R27 000, then the equivalent of US$4 000.

By this time he was married to a white captain in the South African army. As a woman with rank she was protected from the purge, but being forced from the military would lead to a series of events which would ultimately break both Charl and their relationship.

He took a job across the Levubu River as a farm manager for a fraction of the salary. He ran a greenhouse project with his business partner, mostly growing cucumbers and it was there that in happier times their two children were born. But the structure blew down one night in a violent storm leaving them without an income. So with one last roll of the dice, he invested his entire army pension to be part-owner of a hydroponics project at Makhado in the Limpopo Valley, some 450 kilometres north-east of Johannesburg.

It was a state-of-the-art facility built by the French, growing spinach and peppadews for export to Europe. It was run by one of the wives of the Xhosa chief on whose land the project was built. But this enraged the chief's first wife, who was of higher standing under tribal tradition and she got her sons to smash it all down and set her cattle among the peppadews to graze. Overnight, his investment was worthless.

It was during this time that a title claim on the land was lodged by two Venda clans – the Raimondos and Sakumos – under the new government's Restitution of Land Rights Act. It was a programme that mandated the sale of land to those with a rightful claim under government-decreed terms. The Raimondos and Sakumos alleged that their forebears had been forcefully removed to make way for white farmers, something the community strongly contested.

At a public meeting of the Levubu Valley Farmer's Association, 65-year-old Chairman Pieter de Jager declared that he refused to sell his land and a few days later he was murdered by five attackers. His wife and two grandchildren could do nothing but watch him die on the front steps of their farmhouse. He was Charl's neighbour.

Pieter de Jager was one of seven white farmers to be murdered in 2003 and the effect on the community was devastating. Half of them wanted to retaliate, the other half wanted to emigrate. Many eventually sold in desperation, no longer able to stomach finding their cattle felled, hamstrings hacked apart with pangas (machetes) or their sheep lying slaughtered.

In the end they were left with little option but to capitulate and when the farm was sold in 2005, Charl moved the family to nearby Laatsgevonden, owned by Pieter de Jager's son. But times were hard and when the crops died after their water supply was cut off, he too threw in the towel. It was just as Charl and the family were adjusting to their beaten-down wooden shack with its leaking roof and cracked floorboards thanks to an encroaching sycamore tree.

Being uprooted for a second time proved all too much for Charl's wife, who took the kids and went to live with her mother in Pretoria.

Once more, Charl had to pick himself up and start over, this time on his own. He limped through a string of jobs from private security to chauffeuring the owner of a local funeral parlour. As he had no vehicle of his own, Charl had to walk the five kilometres to his house twice a day. He'd truly reached the bottom of the community social ladder, even the farmers he occasionally shared a beer with on Friday nights drove past and left him in their dust. When he fell so ill he couldn't make the journey to work and was fired, he couldn't take it anymore. He had no money, he'd lost his job, his wife, his children, even his dignity.

It was then that a local merchant offered to sell Charl his scrap metal business and when the bank agreed to lend him the R80 000, he couldn't believe his luck. It was his big chance to make something of himself again. Maybe things were finally taking a turn. If he had some money he could afford to pay alimony and if he could pay alimony he could visit his children. That was the deal.

So with permission from the chief, Charl rented a deserted old shop called Charlie's Store adjacent to the scrapyard in a black township called Ga-Matlala Ramoshebo just north of Pretoria. It had no running water and he would be the only white person in the township, but he didn't care. He desperately needed a break. So he packed what few belongings he had and with his Jack Russell Jackie, he headed for Matlala.

Little did he know that the global scrap metal industry was entering its worst slump in history. It was the end of 2008 and spot prices were collapsing, rendering the pile of junk in Charl's new back yard as exactly that.

To this day the bank debt still hangs over Charl's head, except it's inflated to

R200 000. He can barely afford the interest. Looking back at that time, he becomes very introspective. 'To say it was a low point would be a gross understatement,' he says, intently stirring sugar into the fresh cup Liesl put in front of him. As she rubs his shoulder, he takes her hand. 'Dankie, skat.' I could tell there was a great deal more meaning in the thank you gesture.

It's the next day and we're back at the kitchen table. With no room in their house, Charl arranged for me to stay with his neighbour, who was toying with the idea of running a guesthouse on his farm. I was their first customer. We've just finished a breakfast of freshly baked bread with avocado and hot cups of chicory and Charl seems anxious to get on with his story. I sense there's worse to come.

oOo

Lisbet Kgolane lived across the road and a few houses down from Charlie's Store. It was a hot Sunday afternoon when Charl bumped into her that first time on Ga-Matlala's main road. He was on his way to Cash & Carry to buy airtime for his phone, when an Afrikaans-speaking black woman of imposing physique walked right up to him. He recognised her from the little spaza shop she ran from her house, selling cooking oil, maize meal and sweets for the kids.

'What are you doing here?' she demands in Afrikaans.

'I'm going to buy airtime.'

'No, what are you doing *here*?'

'I live here.'

'You cannot live here.' Charl started to get visibly agitated. All he wanted was to get to the shop and this woman was wasting his time. 'Where is your mother?'

'My mother lives on the coast.'

'Then I will be your mother.'

'What are you talking about?'

'God told me I must be your mother.'

'No man, leave me alone.' He stepped around her and on he went.

But Lisbet Kgolane didn't leave him alone. Every time he left his house she came to talk to him and each time the message was the same: God told her she must be his mother. Slowly she wore him down and when he eventually agreed to go to her house for dinner one Sunday evening, she greeted him with a bowl of hot soapy water and a pristine white hand towel over her arm.

'What is this?'

'Keep quiet and wash your hands.' When he had washed, she led him to the head of the table. Then she served him, treating him like he was her own son.

After that Charl went every Sunday and every Sunday she did the same.

It was on one of those evenings that she told him her story. She had been happily married with a two-year-old son and a six-month-old daughter. Then one day her husband left abruptly, returning two weeks later to take everything including the door and windows of their house. Distraught, she collapsed to the ground and prayed. It was then that Jesus appeared to her. He told her He would look after her and that she shouldn't fear for anything, but in return she needed do whatever he told her. She was 21.

Lisbet never remarried. She got a job as a domestic worker in Pretoria and slowly rebuilt the house where her daughter ran a crèche. One Saturday Charl drove them all to a nearby dam in his *bakkie* (small pickup). He made a braai and played football with the children. They still talk about it to this day.

When Lisbet couldn't sleep she'd call him late at night.

'Can you sleep?'

'No.'

'That's because you should be praying.' So they prayed together. Then he started calling her also and slowly, ever so slowly, seeds of self-belief began to sprout. Even though he had no partner, no family, no money and no job, Lisbet Kgolane allowed Charl to remember what it was like to be worth something to someone.

oOo

It was a particularly cold and windy Sunday evening when Charl arrived on Lisbet Kgolane's doorstep to wash his hands for dinner. Lisbet looked around and asked 'Where is your dog?' Jackie went everywhere with him.

'He's sick.'

'What's wrong with him?'

'He's paralysed.'

'Go and fetch the dog. I will pray for him.'

'Don't be mad, you can't pray for a dog.'

'God told me I must.'

'Why?'

'He's your only friend. He will live.'

'He can't walk!'

'He will walk.'

'How can you say that?

'God told me.'

'Okay fine.'

So Charl went home to fetch Jackie. It had been four weeks since he'd seen him barking and scratching under a piece of scrap metal in the yard. A few hours later he noticed him limping and the following morning his hind legs were dragging in the dirt.

Charl took him inside but could do nothing more than make him comfortable. There was no money for a vet and by nightfall all Jackie could move was his head, then not even that. He just lay still, unable to make any sound, unable to eat or drink, just breathing. Charl gave him water through a syringe and fed him little clumps of raw mince, then in the evening he lay him outside to defecate.

He wrapped Jackie in a blanket and walked back over to Lisbet Kgolane's house. As irritated as he was, this was a special day and nothing she could do would ruin it. He'd had a call from a farmer offering him an old plough and at Saturday's scrap market it had fetched exactly enough to pay his alimony. He was finally going to see his children. Perhaps he could even save his marriage. Hope is a very powerful emotion.

He put Jackie down inside the house and Lisbet laid her hands on him and prayed. Then they ate dinner, first serving Charl as she always did.

When he got up to leave, Jackie hadn't moved. So he scooped up the dog irritably and went home. He rose early the next morning, filled his plastic tub with water from the drum and washed, put on a clean shirt and pair of slacks and took the shard of mirror from his dresser drawer to comb his hair by. The drive to Zeerust was five and a half hours and already his hands were shaking.

At his feet Jackie lay dead still. He smiled with mixed emotions. For once he'd wanted nothing more than to be wrong. He scooped up the dog and took it out to the car. Maybe the kids would still want to say hello.

As his bakkie purred along the N1 highway towards Pretoria, Charl heard the patter of teardrops on his cotton shirt but felt nothing. How could it all have come to this? How could his only reason for being depend on the whim of a woman who treated him so badly, yet was supposed to love him most of all? How was it that he needed to look at a picture of his children each morning so he wouldn't slit his wrists? How could the only friend he had in the world be lying lame on his front seat?

He wiped his face with the back of his hand. No, don't go there. Not today. Today is a good day. I am going to see Nikolaas and Hannerie.

Crossing the Apies River, he marvelled at the sun sparkling off the water. He was more than half-way there. Today is a good day. He raised his hands in the air and whooped out loud. He couldn't remember the last time he'd felt so alive. Then, as his bakkie turned off the shallow bridge, all the lights on the dashboard went out and the engine stopped. Charl checked the fuel gauge as the car drifted onto the shoulder and slowly came to a halt. It was three quarters full. No. No. No. Not today. He turned the key. Nothing. Then again. Nothing.

'Fuuuuuuuck,' he screamed. 'Fuck, fuck, fuck, fuck, fuck.' His jaw clenched and his forearms quivered under the strength of his grip as he shook the steering wheel. Not today. Not fucking today. His mouth was completely dry. A dark rage began to infiltrate every fibre of his being, like a fire that first licks at your feet and then slowly engulfs your whole body.

Then, as if in a dream, he remembered the 9mm pistol he kept in the glove compartment. It was there for self-defence, in case he was ever hijacked. He calmly took the gun and checked that it was loaded. After all his military training it was such a natural thing to do. He was on autopilot. Slowly he put the gun to the side of his head. This time he could feel the warm streaks down his cheeks.

He stared out of the windscreen at the empty road ahead. Everything was eerily quiet, like time itself had stopped. He started to squeeze the trigger, but a sudden movement in the corner of his eye made him stop. He turned towards the passenger seat where Jackie had lifted his head and was looking up at him. He let out a little whimper.

No. This isn't happening. Charl jumped out of the car and slammed the door. No, fuck that, it's over. He ran round to the other side of the car and put the gun to his head once more.

He was hyperventilating. He felt the trigger tighten under his finger, but before he could pull it, he had a sudden urge to look down. Jackie had pulled himself up onto the car windowsill with his front paws and was staring at Charl through the passenger window. His tongue hung out of the side of his mouth as he panted heavily.

Charl lowered the gun and slumped to the ground. And there, on that otherwise peaceful Monday morning, he collapsed in a heap beside the Apies River bridge and wept. He wept deeply, soulfully. He wept and wept until he could no longer take the scratching noise coming from inside the car. He reached numbly behind him and opened the door. Jackie came bounding out and jumped on him, licking his face. Licked away the tears. Then ran around in little circles yelping.

A truck pulled up sounding his hooter. Charl waited until the driver grew impatient and left, then pulled himself up and fetched his phone. His uncle arrived from Pretoria within an hour and towed the car to the nearest mechanic. The repairs cost exactly what Charl had in his pocket to pay the alimony. He'd already called his ex-wife, but she had no sympathy for his story. The kids would have to wait and perhaps there was no chance of patching up the marriage after all. So he thanked his uncle and began the long drive home to Ga-Matlala. But not before giving Jackie a bowl of water and a big stick of biltong.

Testing testimony

Riccardo, Liesl's youngest, comes storming into the kitchen. He's every part the quintessential Afrikaner farm boy – short cropped blonde hair and blue eyes, covered head to toe in dirt, upper lip all snot. '*Mama, Mama. Ons is klaar in die tuin. Kan ons nou ons stukkie koek kry, asseblief?*'

He's referring to the scones under a tea towel covered with flies. Liesl rinses a cloth and wipes away the mucus. '*Gaan was eers jou hande. Dan haal jy almal.*' He charges down the hallway to the bathroom and then to call everyone as Liesl watches through watery eyes. At first I think it's because of Riccardo, the kid would make anyone's heart melt. But there is a heaviness to her normally spritely demeanour that indicates otherwise. I wonder then how many times she'd heard that particular story of Charl's.

In a rare moment when we were alone the previous day, I'd asked her if she had heard all of Charl's stories, as he'd just been talking about his military exploits. She said she had, but loved hearing them again because each time there was something a little different, something new. Perhaps it wasn't true for all of them.

'He's one of a kind alright,' I laugh, nodding after Riccardo. It breaks her train of thought. Suddenly she's back in the room, smiling at me.

'He certainly is.' For a moment I succeed in lightening the mood, but Charl has other ideas. He seems wedded to the melancholy, like he wants to get the rest of the story over with. As if reliving it every time brings back too much pain and not just for him. So he launches into the story of the night a big storm hit Ga-Matlala.

Charlie's Store had no ceiling, and with just a few cement bricks pegging the corrugated iron roof to its rafters, it was flimsy at best. So when the brunt of the storm hit just after 8 pm, he knew there was trouble.

At first the roof started to rattle, the wind whistling through it to an ominous crescendo. But with the first big gust one of the corners lifted clean off the wall. Charl jumped up and clung to the nearest rafter to hold it down. He hung on desperately as the roof plucked and pulled, splinters driving into his hands.

The next gust was twice as powerful, ripping the whole roof up except one rafter in a back corner. As it whipped and shook in the howling wind, horizontal rain and sand pelted Charl's face, blinding him. Every muscle in his body was clenched, the veins on his forearms bulging like puppet strings.

'Ok God, if you want to blow me away you do it,' he screamed. 'You do it now. I have nothing left. You win, I don't care anymore.'

He can't recall how long he dangled there, head bowed and blood running down his wrists. But the roof stayed in place and when the storm passed, he collapsed into a heap on his sitting room floor.

The next morning sheets of corrugated iron and structural debris lay strewn across the streets of Ga-Matlala. Charl's carpet was covered in a thick layer of sand.

'That's when I knew my life was no longer my own,' he says staring out of the kitchen doorway. 'That there was some higher purpose.'

He turns to look at me. 'In that moment, hanging there on that rafter, I knew that everything I have, every breath I take, is by God's grace.'

oOo

This wasn't the first time Charl's faith had been tested. Long before moving to Ga-Matlala, one night in their ramshackle house at the bottom of Laatsgevonden farm he was alone with Hannerie when seven men armed with knives and military assault rifles appeared on the doorstep. It was just two months after Pieter de Jager had been murdered.

Hannerie, then just one-and-a-half, was playing in her room, so he slid a kitchen knife in his pocket and ran to confront them outside the house. The only advantage he had was the element of surprise and if he took the fight to them, he might just stand a chance. Gripped by a cold, choking fear, with every step he pleaded with God to protect his daughter.

He stopped one metre away, tightening his grip on the kitchen knife. They were not looking at him, but past him. '*Papa, wat maak jy?*'

His daughter's enquiry about what he was doing scythed through him. The men's bloodlust eyes followed her as she walked up and clutched Charl's leg. She was naked. It is the greatest fear of any father, none more so than in a country notorious for atrocities committed against young children. And on that humid evening, Charl stood paralysed: 'Please God, I know that you exist. Save my daughter. Take my life, do what you want with me, but please just save her.'

As was so often the case, the answer came to him from scripture, this time Romans 12:20: 'If your enemy is hungry, feed him; if he is thirsty, give him something to drink. In doing this, you will heap burning coals on his head.'

Charl calmly picked Hannerie up and propped her on the back of his neck. 'What do you want?' His voice was steady.

'We want money,' came a gruff retort from their leader.

'I don't have money.' Charl regretted it as soon as he spoke the words. They motioned towards him. 'But I have food.' The leader raised his forearm and they stopped.

'We are hungry.'

'Okay, I don't have much, but whatever I have I will give you.' The back of his shorts were damp from the sweat running down his back. 'I'm going into the kitchen to get it, but you have to trust me.' Willing his legs to carry him forward, he reached the kitchen and put Hannerie down. '*Gaan kamer toe and maak die deur toe.*' She obediently went to her room and closed the door. Stuffing half a loaf of bread and three tins of pilchards into a plastic bag, he went back outside and handed it to the leader. 'Like I said it isn't much, but here is all the food I have.'

'Thank you,' said the leader. They turned and left.

Until that attack on the farm, the only thing Charl had to trust was his ability to defend himself. Not a year earlier he'd been mugged late one night at a Johannesburg train station. He had flattened both attackers.

But when his daughter had appeared that humid evening, he was completely in the wilderness. In that moment he was totally and utterly dependent on God's grace and nothing else could save them. This had been the single most defining moment in his spiritual journey. And when the silhouettes of those men disappeared into the dusk, Charl collapsed in a heap on his front doorstep and wept.

It was only much later that he remembered the miracle beside the Sea of Galilee, when Jesus fed the 5 000 with a single loaf of bread and a few fish.

oOo

Despite growing up indoctrinated in a faith, there were many times Charl might have given up, when most of us would have. But God was patient and when he asked for signs they came.

His story is dotted with them.

On the days when he had some money, he'd make instant chicory in his tin cup and sit on the dam wall opposite Charlie's Store, with his Bible in hand. He watched the cattle come in to drink or the doves perch on the branches overhead. Then he'd pray. 'Father, everyone has a mate except for me. Why if even the cattle and the doves can have a mate, why not me?'

Charl met Liesl in 2013. She was happily married to one of his best friends, Willem. He and Willem had worked together in the private security company.

Having wed the first time as a teenager (to upset her parents) Liesl wore the stigma of failed marriage from very early in life. They were children in love and it lasted just as long as the lip gloss.

As is our nature, her next man was entirely the opposite, all flash and brash. But his façade faded with each passing season until all that was left was his abusive nature. By then they had three children. Coupled with the perceived shame of her early failing, she admits to staying far longer than she should have and when she finally plucked up the courage to leave it was time alone that she craved more than anything.

She got to know herself again and for the most part she was happy. But raising three kids alone was a struggle and when a genuine, kind-hearted man came along four years later she was all in. Willem was a good soul and they had a happy and loving marriage, so much so that they decided to have another child of their own, a blessing named Riccardo.

As the years progressed her scars began to fade. But the hopes of a happy and peaceful life were shattered one Spring afternoon when Willem complained of fatigue. At first, Liesl thought it was stress. He'd quit his business and they were living with his family, eleven people in a 3-bedroomed house. But when it persisted, she took him to see an internist and the following day he was diagnosed with advanced cancer throughout his body. He died a week later.

Charl and Liesl had been good friends for five years and after Willem died, he took it upon himself to look after her. What he didn't tell her then was that the night before his death, Willem had appeared to Charl in a dream and asked him to look after Liesl. Charl simply couldn't bring himself to tell her that her best friend and husband was about to die.

Charl prayed for Liesl often. He had a deep urge to be with her, but something was telling him to wait. It was one of the hardest lessons he's ever had to learn.

For days he would turn off his phone so he couldn't contact her, then one morning in early December he couldn't take it anymore. The yearning to reach out to her was too overwhelming. He couldn't stop thinking about her being on her own with four children, with the burden of losing her husband.

'The more I prayed, the more I started thinking about what was going to happen to her,' Charl says. 'I was feeling the deepest, most compassionate love for her as a human being.'

Liesl beams as he relays the phone call.

'Liesl, I have thought and prayed about it. I want to ask you to be my best friend.'

'What are you talking about? I am already your best friend.'

'Yes, but I don't ask my other best friends to marry me.'

Liesl is as vivacious as she is virtuous. It is a rarity for her to be rendered speechless, but that was one such occasion.

'I know this is a lot to process,' Charl said breaking the silence.

'If it's not okay, then you don't have to speak to me again. But I want you to pray about it. And if you can find peace of mind and peace in your heart, then maybe we just take it from there.'

She didn't speak to him for two weeks. Then she called him back and said she was willing to try. So they carried on talking and by the following April she was warming to the idea. 'Can I ask, would you like to visit me?' Charl asked. 'If either of us doesn't feel comfortable, we can scrap the whole idea. But if it feels right, then we can take it one step further.'

My heart swells as it reminds me of the age-old Afrikaner courting tradition. The boy would ask the girl's father if he could visit the family home. If the father was amenable, they would be allowed to sit alone at the kitchen table with a candle in the middle. When it had burnt out, it was time for the boy to go. The longer the candle, the more favour the boy carried.

It would be their ultimate test and their candle kept burning more brightly each day. They got married in July 2019 and Liesl is the first to acknowledge that if Charl hadn't waited, things would never have worked out.

But she'd had signs of her own. She was still close to Willem's mother, who called her late one February afternoon. They were busy discussing a prophetic experience she'd had in church, when she interrupted the conversation and said 'Liesl, I'm sorry but I just need to tell you something. Charl is going to become a very intricate part of your life.' Once more Liesl was floored. 'I have been praying for you and one day God told me. I wanted to let you know I am very happy for you both.' Turned out it was the same day in early December when Charl had put the proposition to her.

Reflecting on that conversation with Willem's mother, Liesl now knows it was the moment she was healed. And it paved the way for their ultimate union.

It was also around that time she developed a deep yearning to have a farm of her own. She didn't grow up on one or even have a particular liking for farming. Rather, she saw it as a place where people could come together to celebrate God, to find community and companionship with fellow believers. Unbeknown to her, the man she had pledged herself to had exactly the same calling. Only Charl being Charl, he needed to hear it much more loudly.

I asked him that after all he'd been through, all the signs and the affirmations, why he believes he is still there. What he believes his purpose to be. He stares out across the barren yard as if searching for the answer. Then his eyes slowly well up and without a word, he pushes back from the table and disappears down the hallway.

'Can I get you some more chicory?' Liesl asks, perhaps to fill the silence.

'Yes. Please.' She turns toward the stove and sparks the gas burner. I hear Charl's boots on the floorboards. He comes bounding in and places two grey stones on the table. They're smooth, oval shapes like those you might find on a beach. In the centre of one is a single white circle. Inside its perfectly round shape are patterns like tiny shadows. He doesn't need to tell me it resembles the moon. On the other is the same pattern, only that one is red. And about half-way around it is a thin red band, like you might see in an eclipse. Apart from being a bit scuffed, they are the only markings on either stone. He slides back into his seat.

'Do you really want to know what my purpose is?' He's more animated now.

'Please. More than you know.'

'I've been using them as door stops.' He picks up one of the stones and rubs it against his shirt. 'Then a week ago I remembered you were coming and suddenly thought I must get some proper ones. But I didn't say anything to Liesl. Then, the very next day, she comes home with two rubber door stops. Man, I tell you, this woman.' He looks over at Liesl drying a cup in the corner. She gives him a coy look over her shoulder. 'I just laughed and gave her a big kiss.'

The light of the moon

Lisbet Kgolane had finally convinced Charl that his future was not in Ga-Matlata. 'God told me that you must go and find your real mother,' she'd said. By then Charl had learned not to argue.

It was 2016 and his divorce had finally gone through. He was 45 and back living with his parents in Bushman's River on the Eastern Cape coast. He described this time as the lowest point in his life. More so than beside the Apies River bridge. His soul was restless, like an itch you just can't reach.

By then he had long adopted the ways of Seventh Day Adventists, thanks to an old army friend who he regularly met up with to read the Bible. He'd convinced Charl that they upheld its fundamental teachings, such as the Sabbath being on a Saturday, one of many similarities with the Jewish faith. One evening, he'd asked Charl when he was planning to keep the feast of Yom Kippur, the Day of Atonement, which marks the end of days of repentance and is considered to be the holiest day in the Jewish calendar. Charl didn't know. That's when he realised that more than anything he needed to find out.

The moon has always been used to set the feast days in the Jewish calendar, its cycles symbolic of the renewal of life. Jews celebrate Rosh Chodesh, 'head of the new moon,' to mark the start of each new lunar month. In ancient times Rosh Chodesh was declared by the Jewish court only after two credible witnesses would testify that they had seen the first sliver.

Charl used to sit with his son Nikolaas and wait for the crescent to appear to celebrate the start of a new month. To find hope in its renewal, in what might lie ahead. But something had always bothered him about the ritual. Now he realised that this was his sole mission. He needed to get clarity. It was a burning desire from the deepest cavern of his being, so momentous he couldn't get a grip on it.

A storm had set in, waves hammering the banks of the Boesman's River. Charl couldn't sleep, so just after daybreak he ran down to the river mouth, looking out over the churning sea. He walked aimlessly along the beach praying 'Please, please Father, if you are really real, if you love me like you say you do ... if you have compassion on humanity. I am not worthy of a sign, I don't want to ask for a sign, but if you just show yourself to me ...'

He stopped in his tracks. At his feet was a pattern in the sand, the width of two feet and of breathtaking beauty, intricate formations sculpted by the wind and tide in an array of melting colours. He followed the pattern along the water's edge until it suddenly turned 90 degrees from the shoreline towards the sand dunes. He stood puzzled. There was no conceivable reason for such a change in course. So he followed the pattern over the dunes, into an open area the size of a half a football field, covered entirely with stones. Exhausted, he stumbled into the middle and scraped away an area big enough to lie down. Then he covered his head and fell asleep, for what might have been centuries.

When he woke up, his arms were spread wide to the sides, his legs together as if nailed to a cross. A voice told him to look to his left. There next to his hand was a single stone. He picked it up and marvelled at the perfect full moon in its centre. Then the voice said, 'Now look to your right.' So he turned his head and there, next to his other hand, was a second stone. In its centre was a perfect blood moon, surrounded by a half crescent.

Charl sat upright and stared at the stones in his hands. Then he got up and ran back to the house to find his Bible. He thumbed frantically through the pages until he found Psalm 81:3 which he read aloud: 'Sound the ram's horn at the new moon and when the moon is full, on the day of our festival; this is a decree for Israel, an ordinance of the God of Jacob.'

He fell back on his bed and laughed, his heart overflowing with joy. Tears flowed down the cracks of his weathered face as if to clear them away. He felt humbled to be alive, bursting with grace. He would test his faith no more.

oOo

'So you ask me, what is my purpose?' Now Charl is smiling, the subtle crease of crows' feet accentuating his lively eyes once more. I simply nod, not wanting to disrupt his flow. 'Some translations of the Bible say new moon, some say full moon,' he continues. 'Some people keep the full moon as the first day of the new month, some the dark moon. The problem with the dark moon is, you cannot see it. Our Father is the father of light. Scripture says it's there not just for light, but for signs and seasons. The moon, sun and stars were created to give us the calendar, the feast days and to distinguish between day and night, between light and dark, between good and evil. Jesus's crucifixion was on a High Sabbath which aligns perfectly with the cycle of the full moon. It just has to be the full moon we celebrate.' He's worked up now and I have never seen him this enlivened.

'Now that I know, it's like a fire that burns inside me. I simply cannot be untrue to it. There are many that will fight me on this, but I cannot ignore it. It is my mission to share it, so that people can understand.' He pauses for breath. Liesl is rapt. She's sitting quietly across the table, hands neatly folded on her lap. It's a rare moment of stillness in her otherwise frenetic day. There is admiration in the way she looks at him, the deepest kind of love and respect. 'People don't want to hear that they are keeping the Sabbath on the wrong day, or that they are celebrating the feasts on the wrong dates. But it's a cross that I must bear.' For a moment I think of Charl hanging from the rafters that day of the big storm and lying in the valley of stones.

'Most of us are spiritually blind. Only by crying out and asking for guidance, by putting our own interests to one side, only then are we ready to be helped; to be shown the truth. If I didn't go through the journey I did, I wouldn't have been brought to such a state of complete understanding that I am nothing. Nothing, nothing, nothing. If the things that happened didn't erode all these false hopes and false beliefs as a human being, then I wouldn't have received this. It's not about me anymore, it just cannot be.'

And now we get to the crux of it. Charl talks about owning a farm one day. Liesl is upright in her chair, like a meerkat. He speaks of their plan to create an environment where people can come from all around to share in God's word. Where anyone can come and put up a tent without judgement. Where they can share and learn and celebrate the feasts of the full moon.

'All we need is a farm,' he smiles. 'No matter how impossible it seems, I know one day it will happen.' Liesl walks around the table and embraces him. They look at each other.

'It will happen,' she says. 'We just need to keep believing.'

oOo

In moments when we'd been alone, Liesl and Charl had both said how special my visit had been, but I couldn't understand why. It was only some days later when I was long gone that it dawned on me. I was a visitor from a strange land. I had travelled across the world to be with them in their space. To hear their story, to celebrate with them the power and love of God. Perhaps it was a taste of what they both so deeply desired. I hoped there would be many more after me.

Not black and white

It's our last night together and Charl and I are driving back from the nearest shop with supplies for a braai. In true Afrikaner tradition they wanted to give me a good send-off, plus it's a rare treat for the kids. I stopped him as he headed for the cash dispenser to draw some money – it was the least I could do and it broke my heart to see the relief on his face when I offered to pay.

It is a proud thing to be an Afrikaner. Their love of country and sense of duty to defend it is surpassed only by their familial bonds. The need to protect and provide for their kin is as deeply engrained in their psyche as the first ox-wagon wheels that cut the trails to trek to the Eastern Cape. To rob a man of this right is to rob him of his soul and in all our conversations, the pain that Charl felt most was losing this right.

It is as honourable as the fact that despite everything that has happened to him, Charl never felt resentful towards black people. 'Ultimately it's not about being a Boer or a Brit or a Xhosa or a Zulu. It's about being a child of God,' he says staring at the hills in the distance. 'We have different nations, peoples, cultures and traditions, but through the love of Christ we can look past that and move towards a future. A future where there is peace, there is respect and there is brotherly love.'

His words trail off as if he knows it's an unattainable dream. More than anything, he yearns to see the country he loves realise its true potential. To have a justice system that rightly and fairly brings to order those that choose to break the law. To have its state-owned enterprises run by true public servants appointed on merit.

He thinks there is a strong willingness on both sides of the racial divide to make things work, but popular politics have the potential to destroy that goodwill, even lead to civil war. A bill allowing expropriation of land without compensation has been pushed through parliament and there's nothing he or his people can do about it. It will start with their farms, but where does it end?

The current South African government has already acquired more than 4 600 farms he tells me, mostly funded by foreign donors for the purposes of land restitution. Before this, land which had been expropriated by the Afrikaner government under apartheid and belonged to generations of white farmers, had been handed back to their rightful owners. He was referring to all the land between the Great Fish and the Kei rivers, the whole of the former Ciskei region.

'Most of it has gone to waste,' Charl says. 'Many of the black people they offered the land to didn't know how to farm so they took the money instead. Of course, no-one talks about that. But humanity can feel good about itself now because everything has been put to rights. The British, Americans and Australians can all feel better about themselves, because they can legitimately point the finger at South Africa and deflect their own misgivings.'

He's not wrong. I now live in a country where native Aboriginal people are still not recognised in the constitution. That's perhaps more difficult to comprehend than legalising racial segregation.

But what's far more troubling is Charl's concerns about South Africa's future. 'There are many people who stand to benefit from a civil war in South Africa,' he says. We're back in the kitchen, a flurry of moths perhaps aptly crashing into the single exposed light bulb hanging from the ceiling. He's rubbing the seasoning into some lamb chops. 'People are fed-up. The frequent droughts, livestock theft, rising cost of labour and now even the water rights.' He's referring to water being reallocated by the State according to land mass and population demographics, rather than agricultural productivity.

'The farmers are prepared to fight for what they believe is rightfully theirs. And any attempt to remove their right to bear arms will be ignored,' he says. He's talking about the tightening gun legislation, although with crime rates where they are this is surely a blessing. 'The world needs to take cognisance of what is happening in South Africa. Farmers are still being murdered. It has to stop and the current government needs to bring those responsible to justice.' He pauses as if forgetting what he's meant to be doing. Then he looks at me.

'We have nothing more to lose. Those who wanted to leave have left and the rest cannot afford to. We have built up this country and now they want to take it from us. If they do, there will be war.' He gets teary when he says his people have every right to be there and no-one can make him leave. As one of the many South Africans who chose the latter option several years ago, it sparks a tinge of personal remorse to have left behind the only land where I can truly say its soil runs in my veins.

His people just want to be left alone, to restore their culture and to govern themselves. Having been in the military for a decade, he is the last person to advocate for a fight. But in the absence of any other options, he will support his comrades to the end if he has to.

His tone suddenly shifts. He looks up at me and smiles, as if buoyed by a new thought. Ironically, he says, this next chapter in the country's history may finally give him the opportunity to buy his farm: to fulfil his lifelong dream and now that of his loving new wife. Still laden with debt, he has no idea how it will transpire, but he sees it as the ultimate act of faith.

oOo

As I edge over the top of the hill in my Volkswagen rental to navigate the rutted farm roads back to civilisation, I glance in my rear-view mirror once more. Charl, Liesl and the kids are still standing at the gate, giving me one last wave. On the back seat wrapped in kitchen towel are some of Liesl's muffins and their last pack of chicory from the pantry. My argument against taking it had been in vain.

As soon as I am out of sight I pull over. I'm not quite ready to leave this place, so I sit for a while and soak in the stark beauty of the valley below, with its smattering of green gwarrie and schotia trees and even the occasional prickly pear cactus. The stillness is soothing.

I wonder, were I this son of a priest put through such times, how would I have shaped up? Would I have been so virtuous? Could I have remained so humble? Would I have come out the other side with such conviction in my faith?

Just then I remember the story of the hoopoe bird. Charl and Liesl moving into the small green farmhouse had been an extremely testing time. Bringing two families together is never easy, especially under those circumstances. Each night they had prayed for things to work out, to get better. Then one Saturday morning as they lay in bed, they heard a bird call. 'Hoop … hoop.' And again 'Hoop … hoop.' They looked at each other and burst out laughing.

Charl followed the sound around the outside of the house and found the little orange-crested bird with its distinctive black and white feathers building a nest behind the water tank, just below their bedroom window. And for the next few months until the chicks had hatched and flown away, it was their daily wake up call. 'Hoop … hoop.' It filled their hearts and put a spring in their step, because they knew God was there watching over them.

Hoop in Afrikaans means 'hope'.

oOo

Charl had every reason to feel resentment towards indigenous people in South Africa, as did they towards him. It's one of many scars from the country's colourful history. Yet he never saw the hardships inflicted on him and his family as a race issue and all he strives for is the fair and equitable treatment of all South Africans. Because despite a fierce intellect, he is a man guided by his heart not his head and were all the country's people that way inclined it would be in a very different state.

Like me, he is a man whose views had been moulded by the constructs of the Church, yet his own path lay indistinguishably in his father's shadow. Our fathers had instilled in us the same moral guardrails needed to chart our course, but it was only in discovering our own purpose that we could find truth in the pages of the Holy Bible, in both languages.

Charl is a man who just wants to provide for his family. It's why my empathy runs deeper still with each passing day he remains estranged from his son and daughter because of an inability to provide for them. For years he has wandered in the wilderness, been mocked and beaten while carrying his people's cross until he reached the point of complete surrender. Yet he remains unwavering in his belief that God will provide for both him and his children, because no matter how much he was broken down, no-one could take away his faith.

How admirable is it that in the face of such hardship he can still find hope? One of the many verses underlined in ballpoint in the well-worn Bible that's permanently on the kitchen sideboard is Isaiah 40:31, 'But those who hope in the Lord will renew their strength. They will soar on wings like eagles; they will run and not grow weary, they will walk and not be faint.' It's one of his favourites, which he often reads to his children when they visit the small Eastern Cape farmhouse with its olive-green walls.

But above all else, Charl is a decent and honourable man, whose greatest desire is to have a piece of land in the country he loves to call his own, where he can do God's work in communion with any of his fellow South Africans who choose to be there. This is his purpose. And it is on this hope that he will soar like an eagle until he realises his dream.

12
Victoria's privilege

Victoria Veronica Mills grew up in Sydney's prestigious Northern Beaches. From the outside, her life would have been the envy of many: a student at a prestigious local Catholic School, views across the Pacific in a Bilgola beach house she shared with her older brother and well-respected parents. Even a shiny black Labrador. By all accounts they were a perfect cookie-cutter family.

But behind the façade, the world she lived in was one of isolation, displacement and loneliness. It was a world created by the magical fantasies of a juvenile mind and the only place she felt safe and protected, the only place she could breathe.

Behind the walls of their pristine Bilgola home lay a dark secret that would steal her youth and alter the course of her life forever.

Victoria's most vivid childhood memory is running into the pub to fetch her dad for dinner, while her mum waited anxiously in the idling car. She describes the reek of beer as he slumped into the front seat, disheveled and disinterested. It was the same smell that would so often follow him into her bedroom at night.

She remembers the car especially, a white VW Beetle. Not because she liked driving in it, but because some strange men arrived one day to take it away. He'd lost it on the horses, no money chasing bad. The by-product of being an addict on every level – gambling, booze, drugs, sex.

When you're five years old you simply don't have the ability to comprehend what is happening in the dark of night by a trusted parent. Or the vocabulary to tell anyone. She coped by disassociating from herself. Her soul split from her tiny body, a puppet in her father's prying hands. Maybe someone would see her pain. But her mother put it down to anxiety and remained blind to it for another three decades.

'I can't say my childhood was filled with lots of wonderful happy memories,' Victoria tells me while sipping a cup of hot tea. She looks up from across the small white table in my Manly apartment in Sydney's Northern Beaches not far from where she grew up. Her eyes shimmer as the afternoon light reflects in her welling tears. They're a striking blue, even against the backdrop of the ocean through the bi-fold doors behind her. A tear escapes and tumbles down her tanned cheek. At 49, the features that saw her crowned Ms New South Wales are as prominent as ever – a blonde bob frames her high cheekbones and defined jawline. But while she still portrays an immaculate image, she has long since shed any attachment to ego. Her long journey to find self-love is complete, through a steadfast connection with God.

She was 34 when she finally found the courage to confide in her mother – that for years she'd suffered abuse at the hands of her father. Judith Mills broke down in tears. She had an old-school elegance about her that was well-suited to her trim blonde features, but she was also deeply soulful and philosophical. Neither side could comprehend the atrocity confronting her.

Through unabating tears Victoria talked about those nights alone in her bedroom; how the fear of her father coming in was sometimes even worse. About how she emptied his beer bottles at night so he wouldn't be drunk. It was her way of pacifying him.

Judith's apologies were deeply soulful. Victoria simply took her hand and they embraced, as if for the first time. While they'd developed a bond over the years, the undercurrent of silence had run deep.

She believed that her mother had no idea of the abuse that took place, and that she'd just been trying to survive herself, navigating a toxic marriage and raising two kids and a sick husband. She accepted that her mother had done her best.

The truth would unfurl a love that Victoria had always dreamed of sharing with her mother. There was a lot of catching up to do and all those years of blame for not protecting her vanished like a watercolour in the rain. It's what makes Victoria such a remarkable human.

It would be the beginning of a healing process that saw them become best friends, until cancer took Judith suddenly. 'I finally got the chance to know her for who she was without the grip of my father being around,' Victoria says. 'It was so beautiful and sad at the same time. She died far too young.'

They were due to fly out to Koh Samui in Thailand for a holiday. Judith had been complaining of back pains, so Victoria forced her to go and get it checked. 72 hours later she was diagnosed with stage four bowel cancer which had spread to her liver and stomach. She collapsed in Victoria's home and was rushed to hospital where they operated straight away, removing a tumour the size of a grapefruit. She passed away thirteen weeks later. 'I miss her every day,' Victoria says quietly.

A model life

Robert (Bob) Mills considered himself a man of influence. Growing up in Bankstown on the wrong side of the tracks, he'd left school to become a court reporter and help his family. Chiselled dark features lent him an air of confidence that alongside a youthful charisma saw him rub shoulders with judges and barristers from an early age. He made it his business to know those who would serve him well. But he was also a bitter and angry man. The vices were his way of coping.

Victoria recalls him going in and out of rehabilitation centres half a dozen times. 'He tried to fix himself,' she says. 'But he was trying so hard to kill the demons through gambling and drink that he couldn't change his behaviour.'

Endless affairs meant Bob was rarely at home. Judith dealt with it by moving the family around. Relocating to Adelaide, Hobart and Canberra before eventually returning to Sydney. But across each new threshold were the same dashed hopes of a fresh start. All that flourished was her father's alcoholism, which defined Victoria's teenage years. Years she wishes she could forget.

Attending seven different schools across five states meant she couldn't settle anywhere for long enough to build lasting friendships, so she stopped trying. It was easier than leaving them behind. The instability added more bricks to the emotional wall around her heart and intensified her isolation. There was no one to trust, nowhere that she belonged. It would lead to a string of unhealthy relationships as she tried harder and harder to find approval and validation. To feel like she was loveable.

It's no wonder then that she immersed herself in modelling to escape, to find some sense of identity. What started out as a way to make money while she was still at school soon blossomed into a budding career that took her around the world. She landed a lucrative contract with Image modelling agency in Tokyo, where she launched herself on the party lifestyle. Living at a hundred miles an hour, she was seen at Tokyo's trendiest clubs, bars and restaurants.

But rather than remind her of who she was, it sucked her into a superficial world that brought pockets of fulfillment in shiny wrappers. 'It was a completely dehumanising experience,' she says. 'I'd never felt more alone, more removed from what was real.'

Beneath the mascara and fancy clothes grew a deep-rooted and dark depression. And a yearning to help others, to be of service in some way. She believed that it was only by helping other people that she could fill the void inside her.

So when she was crowned Ms New South Wales in 1992 and was asked to endorse a national disability centre charity, she embraced the opportunity. She travelled across the country to elevate awareness of cerebral palsy and she finally felt like she had a useful role in society. But it was just another mask for her self-loathing and pain. She was trying to outrun herself, to reinvent who she was, but now with paper and glue.

Too afraid to turn around, she kept pushing harder. She joined Vogue as a stylist and worked her way up to an executive role. Then she moved to Clarins where she became director of public relations. She worked hard and played harder, luxuriating in the fast money, fast cars and fast friends, exuding an image of ultra-confidence, a young woman with the world at her fingertips.

Once again, she mistook her outward success for a stable and fulfilling existence. But the faster she ran, the deeper grew the cracks of discontent. The warning signs began to take their toll in exhaustion, fatigue, and repetitive headaches. Even three car accidents in a handful of months wasn't enough to make her stop, until the façade came crashing down like a fallen chandelier, splintering across the hospital floor where she lay. It would be the first of two bouts of meningitis or acute inflammation of the brain. The problem was, it forced her to stop and to think. To look in the tainted rear-view mirror.

'I realised my life was a total mess,' she says. 'I was lying alone in hospital, completely disconnected from myself. The emotional pain from not dealing with the trauma had taken its toll. I was 28 years old and staring into the abyss.'

Victoria looks down at her manicured hands. Nowadays she just takes care of herself because it feels good. But there's a pensiveness about her, like she doesn't often talk about that time, as if she's back on that hospital bed contemplating giving up. Then she looks right at me, eyes clear as crystal.

'That's when I encountered God for the first time,' she says. Suddenly she relaxes into the translucent Philippe Stark dining chair. The soft glow that seems always to surround her returns.

'It was as clear as day, like someone was in the room with me. "It's not your time," the voice said. It filled the whole room. I looked around but there was no-one there.' As much as she wanted to fight hearing those words, she knew exactly what it meant. That she had a different purpose on the planet and that there was no time for self-pity. That she needed to get well and get on with the job of being of service.

Until then she'd had a concept of God. She'd always sensed His presence, but had been too consumed with her own misery to let Him in. Trailing her mother and brother to church growing up had been more chore that choice. Staid Catholic priests espousing God in their formulaic ways had pushed her away rather than create any meaningful connection. What she needed was a direct dial.

'That day in the hospital was the turning point,' she says brightly.

oOo

Returning home after that first bout of meningitis, perhaps in denial or still angry at the thought of having to keep going, Victoria started losing herself again in late night parties. Trying once again to self-medicate, like she wasn't ready to heed the lessons life was trying to teach her. She fell into the same vacuous traps and toxic relationships.

On a blind date she met a man she believed to be a kindred spirit – good looks, a successful career, a fierce will to succeed and a childhood beset with an alcoholic father. Once again, she thought the relationship would rescue her, but like the string of men before him it was only her sparkly exterior he craved. A superficially perfect woman to set up their superficially perfect home and to mask his own deep-rooted issues.

Three months into their stormy relationship Victoria fell pregnant. There is a liveliness about her each time she speaks of Noah, her only child. 'I saw it clear as day in the corner of the room, like the universe exploding,' she says. 'I knew instantly it was a child that needed to be born.'

Her message to the father was clear – she was bringing her son into the world with or without him and to his credit he vowed to support them. But not long after the shotgun wedding, nestled in the bosom of their pristine new Balmain home, his true colours came out like rainbows at Mardi Gras.

'Turned out he was an exact replica of my father,' Victoria says somberly. 'He was an obsessive gambler and an abusive drunk with a fiery temper.' She knew she had to start plotting an exit. Watching the signs, Noah never settled. From the moment he was born he cried incessantly. Overcome by sleep deprivation and denied the baby bliss she so desperately craved, Victoria knew something was intrinsically wrong. 'It was more than post-natal depression,' she says. 'I came to realise that the problem wasn't Noah. His unhappiness was just an extension of my own. I had become the world's greatest actor, parading around in a mask pretending everything was okay and that my life was perfect.'

Recognising the emotional pain she was in, it was then that a girlfriend connected her with an experienced life coach, a seemingly small gesture that would transform her life. She came to understand for the first time that through controlling her thoughts, by taking action and sticking to a plan she could create meaningful change.

'Instead of going to another counsellor to talk about my feelings, the coaching gave me tangible solutions and strategies to fix the mess. It was a total epiphany,' she says. 'At the same time Noah was my greatest wake-up call. I needed a calm and peaceful environment to raise him. The coaching gave me what I needed to build a different life for us both.'

No longer making changes just for herself, it drove her to find a solution to her most deep-rooted issues and equipped her to start making better choices and breaking old patterns. Less than 12 months later, she left her marriage. Baby on her hip and suitcase in hand, Judith couldn't help her out of the door fast enough. And in the clearing rear-view mirror she began to recognise the person, colleague, friend, daughter, sister and mother she always wanted to be.

'I was so empowered by the coaching I just knew it was my calling,' she smiles. 'I was totally mesmerised by how simple but effective it was. I knew in my heart it was my true purpose, that it was how I could make a real difference in this world and give this gift to others.'

With a helping hand from her mother, she threw everything at upskilling herself – counselling, NLP, joining the International Coaching Federation. She wasn't inspired by self-help books precisely because they were so uninspiring. 'I have zero respect for anyone who hasn't been through their own journey who then coach others,' she says reflecting on those early years. 'They just don't have the compassion or empathy, the same relatability nor wisdom.'

Combined with her experience in business, marketing and PR, by the time Noah was two she had started her own coaching company. Over the next 20 years it became a global success story helping countless Fortune 500 executives, celebrities, business owners, entrepreneurs and individuals from all walks of life. 'It was a profoundly powerful time,' Victoria says. 'I knew that I needed to dedicate my life to helping others heal their broken hearts, to give them a roadmap. When you finally understand your purpose, it's a total game changer.'

As she says it, I can't help feeling that our lives are intertwined, only she's driving and I've slipped into the back seat. I wonder how it is that so many people may not even consider their purpose and others spend their lives feeling like something is missing but never act on it.

Mike's death sparked in me a deep curiosity to understand my purpose. It was only in discovering it years later that I could understand that all it took was to ask the right questions. Because it's only when we take the time to ask that we can find our way to the truth. And when we know, we wonder how we could have gone for so long without it. Buddha said 'Your purpose in life is to find your purpose and give your whole heart and soul to it ... those who have failed to work toward the truth have missed the purpose of living.'

Painful reflections

Victoria's eventual revelation to her mother was a watershed moment for them both. Everything instantly fell into place for Judith, like a lifting fog. Victoria's shutting down as a child, her depression, bitter anger and her lengthy illnesses.

It suddenly made sense why all the best doctors and therapists she had thrown money at couldn't diagnose her child. Because what she suffered from was a broken heart, a heart too young to know how to deal with the trauma and betrayal.

Judith finally understood her husband, too. His constant struggle with life and his deep-rooted anger. It was then she revealed to Victoria that Bob had been abused as a Catholic altar boy from the ages of six to eleven.

She was floored. The parallels were staggering. While it gave her some understanding of the forces that drove her father's choices, it was no excuse. She believed he knew that what he was doing was wrong. But understanding that he'd endured the same pain and humiliation had opened the door of compassion just wide enough to let in a sliver of light.

When Victoria confronted her father not long after, Judith made sure she was by her side. The two women sat across the table from a man they had spent their lives with but whom neither really knew.

Victoria placed two photographs in front of her father. One of herself at the age of five, the other of him as a young altar boy. Clutching her mother's hand, she let it all out, reliving her childhood, tear by painful tear. No tears were returned. Her father listened stone-faced and pleaded the Fifth: the man somehow couldn't remember, nor find it in his heart to apologise.

But his denial was of no consequence. Victoria needed to release the pain – all those years of guilt, shame and self-destruction because it's all she believed she was worth. It was time to choose to love who she was for the first time. It was time to release the hold her father had had over her since she was five. To cut the puppet strings and bring light into the darkness.

When she'd finished, she handed him a letter. She'd written it all down in case she couldn't follow through. It was clinical and methodical. Then, in that same moment, she told him she loved him.

For a while Victoria stares out at some passing sailboats. The afternoon breeze has picked up, ruffling the normally calm waters of North Harbour. Fathers and their children duck under swinging beams as they change tack. You could almost hear their laughter. 'I can't imagine how painful it must have been for Mum to go through that,' she says as if speaking to them. Once again, she's thinking of others and thinking as a mother. I try to reconcile the bitter-sweet triumph, how it must have felt to finally have the truth acknowledged only to be faced with more lies.

But as much as it was beyond my comprehension, the impact of confronting her father had repercussions far worse than Victoria had feared. It cracked open the vault that had kept her trauma locked inside for all those years. And as the pain and anguish re-surfaced, so did the symptoms – lesions, seizures, migraines, memory loss, chronic fatigue, hair loss. Like long lost friends coming back to play.

Meanwhile, juggling parenting duties and coping with expanding her international business, the demands on her time once again spiraled out of control. Although this time justifiably – she had a career she was passionate about and a profound love for her son. But the faster the hamster wheel turned, the more she feared stopping. Until once again it was stopped for her, only with far more severe consequences.

Victoria was diagnosed with cerebral lupus and told her quality of life would deteriorate rapidly over the next two years, if she survived that long. A form of autoimmune disease, her body had been systematically attacking her own tissues and organs, in this case her brain. 'I think my body was trying really hard to tell me to stop living in my brain and start living in my heart,' she said. 'I had disconnected so much from my heart as a way to reduce feeling anything. It was so full of toxic thoughts and beliefs that it created these immense energetic blocks.' All those years of running away had finally caught up with her.

The doctors prescribed protocols to control the symptoms and to try and reboot her brain. But she knew deep inside that what she needed was something much more radical. She needed to address the root cause, to reconnect with herself. That wasn't going to happen in a hospital ward. So she refused and started a personal healing journey to finally deal with her trauma head-on.

She closed her business and called in favors to help look after Noah, then boarded a plane for India. For the next few months, she was in and out of an Ayurvedic clinic, a defibrillator for her body, mind and soul. 'I went on my own Eat, Pray, Love mission,' she laughs.

She discarded anything that was negative – thoughts, friends, behaviours. She went vegan and engaged in the best medical care, both eastern and western including integrative practitioners, naturopaths and nutritionists. 'My life was on the line and Noah's too. I had to strip away everything that was not of God's doing and rebuild my relationship. I needed to ask for help.'

She started working with her own coaches, to keep her accountable and inspired when she felt like giving up. It would be the backbone of her healing to bring all of who she was into a complete state of wellness. Seven hours a day of detox, yoga, meditation and spiritual work.

As a teenager she'd grown up practicing Transcendental Meditation with her parents but had lost time for it. So she dived back in, practicing twice a day among levitating monks. 'It was a profoundly powerful experience,' she smiles. 'It was exactly where I needed to be. As humans we go down directions not part of the greater good, but we can change that. Before then I hadn't been willing to surrender and to let God make the decisions that I wasn't able to make.'

She learned to listen to herself again, learned to trust herself. She did things that made her laugh, took long walks, slept late and napped in the afternoons. And over countless cups of tea she learned to forgive, both herself and her father.

'It took nearly thirty years to forgive Dad,' she says. But there's a distinct airiness to her demeanour now, as if remembering a burden long since discarded. 'I just needed to deal with all the garbage first. I needed to heal and get back into flow. Being given two years to live when you have a four-year-old son can really change your perspective. I was determined not to let my father screw up my entire life.'

oOo

For Judith, finally knowing the truth had given her the escape she'd secretly craved. The veneer of pretence could finally come down and she could leave the loveless marriage she'd worked so tirelessly to protect.

For nearly 20 years Victoria had been pleading with her to leave her father. Now at 60 years old she finally had the chance at a new start. It's what made her sudden death that much crueler. 'She was my best friend, my shining light,' Victoria says. 'When you've been carrying around such a heavy heart for so long, the darkness will eventually find you.'

Victoria began respecting her mother in earnest after Noah was born. She had been like a second mother to him and a rock to Victoria. She helped her navigate single parenting, looking after Noah when she had to travel and showered them both with love and affection. So the minute Judith was diagnosed, they both cared for her until the end. It gave Victoria the time to say things she needed to and her mother the grace and dignity she'd earned.

Until her illness became too much, Judith would occasionally still visit Bob. And three months after she passed away, he followed her to the grave. 'My father died of a broken heart,' Victoria says. 'He couldn't be on the planet without Mum. He couldn't bear the guilt and shame anymore.' There is no bitterness when she says it. Rather, it is genuine heartfelt sorrow. To have lost them both so early and to be abandoned once more.

Half an hour before he died, Bob had tried to call Victoria and her brother Scott but neither of them answered. From the day she'd confronted her father he would play no further part in her life. She'd set clear boundaries to provide the space to heal.

When the hospital called to say he'd had a heart attack, Scott had implored Victoria to go and see him but there was nothing she needed to hear from her father. The final call came just half an hour later. Victoria wept, but they were tears of relief, not sorrow. Relief to be finally free of his physical presence in this world.

After that day her relationship with Scott shut down. All she can surmise is that he blames her for their parents' separation. Shortly after the showdown with her father, Judith had filed for divorce after a 40-year-long marriage. 'My brother doesn't want to hear the truth about what Dad did,' Victoria says. 'His way of coping is out of sight, out of mind. It's the only explanation.'

I reflect on my three siblings and the incredible relationship we have. The love we share and how much we have all drawn from and depended on one another. To have just one and then lose them is unfathomable.

I think about the phone call she didn't take from her father and what the conversation might have been like if she'd answered.

'Do you ever think about it?' I ask Victoria.

'Of course I do,' she says. 'Often. Maybe it would have been his come to Jesus moment.' Then she looks straight at me. 'But I didn't.'

Cause and effect

Victoria now knows the decision to forego the medical protocols was part of God's plan, as was everything else. Had she stopped long enough to catch the cerebral lupus early, had she not gone on her spiritual journey, she wouldn't have recognised and studied the connected relationships between our mind, body, spirit, emotions and energetic fields. In India 'disease' is how they describe the body's way of crying out for radical realignment.

Recovering from childbirth, a newborn baby, dysfunctional marriage and an abusive partner had simply demanded too much of her time to recognise her more deep-rooted issues.

And it was following this healing system that would shape her life for the next 20 years. By going into the vault and dealing with every aspect of her trauma.

Ironically, it's now her father she relies on as a spiritual guide. 'I see him a lot and feel his presence close to me,' Victoria says, looking around the room. 'The spiritual version is much better,' she laughs.

I'm suddenly overcome by emotion as I think about Mike Fisher. I rarely tell his story because it's so deeply personal, but when I do I struggle not to lose my voice. Each time I have chosen to share it, though, it has been with purpose. And I know it has helped others on their spiritual journeys also. It's the only way I can justify him dying so young. We can never know the impact we have on other people, all we can do is try and live a life of example. And I know that in death Mike is happy that he continues to touch the lives of many people he's never even met.

Victoria knows that her father is proud of what she's doing, even though she never heard him say the words while he was still around. 'He couldn't tell me because he was captive to his own demons. But when I tap into him at a psychic level I can feel his love. He's finally free of his human addictions,' she says.

It's the culmination of many years of discovering her spiritual gift, one that has perpetuated prophetic visions and not always welcome ones. It has given her psychic abilities to understand and know people, to see their life paths and understand their thoughts. All pretty handy when pursuing a career as a coach.

But there were some things she still remained blind to, perhaps out of a subconscious desire for Noah to have a father figure in his life. She fell into another long-term relationship, this time with Craig, a fellow divorcee who paraded as a media personality, regularly appearing on daytime television and writing financial columns for national papers.

Like Sleeping Beauty, for years she was enchanted by his persuasive ways and by their fairy-tale lifestyle. She believed she had forged a happy home for them both and had created a wholesome environment for Noah and his children, and that she no longer had to go it alone. She allowed herself to trust again, to love again. It would be one final roll of the dice and she was all in.

The more desperately she clung to the ideal, the more she forgave her partner's destructive behaviours, blind to his infidelity. But the betrayals were just a part of it.

In 2019, the Australian Royal Commission into the financial services industry exposed him publicly and she was forced to witness his fantastic web of lies and deceit in the same newspapers he'd used to orchestrate it.

Their life as they knew it started to unravel. Instead of accepting responsibility for his actions, Craig fell straight into the arms of another woman, betraying Victoria and the family they had raised. Suddenly all the things she believed they both held in such high regard lay shattered around her. Left with a broken heart, broken family, broken friendships and broken truths, she was inconsolable. 'I really trusted him,' she says. 'It was to be my final lesson. A man is never a plan.'

It made her realise how much she'd compromised her values and taken her eye off the commitment to her life calling. The deceit and betrayal, of her as well as Noah, ignited in her the clarity, vision and burning need to build something that would forever empower other women. It's what led to the birth of Hello Coach, a platform connecting people with life coaches around the world.

'I meditated and prayed every day,' she says. 'When things ended with Craig, the vision suddenly became so clear. Literally in a handful of days I knew I had to help heal people's hearts to let the light in and that it was time to step up and realise this vision without any further distractions. Having your heart broken apart in a thousand different ways gives you compassion and the ability to relate to people's pain points. It equipped me to create a global voice of change.'

It's a bold vision and never has she been more animated, nor more motivated. She understands, too, that the coaching business she built over 20 years was a mere stepping stone.

'All these incredible expert coaches represent different pillars of life,' she explains. 'Spiritual, physical, emotional, cognitive, energetic. You take what you need.' Having been on that journey herself, she understands the power that lies in her hands.

Naturally, it's also the culmination of another path to forgiveness. This time of Craig. 'Had I not gone through it all, I wouldn't have had the need to create Hello Coach,' she says wistfully. 'I am grateful for that period of my life, grateful for what I learned from him. I have full forgiveness for him. He put me through hell, but you just have to keep looking for the silver lining.'

It forced her once again to look at her belief structures and judgements, the perception of who she was. To find the path to self-love. 'The journey of growth is to strip back who you think you are and to find out who you really are,' she says. 'We are all part of God. And the only way to know it is to have the experience of God in our lives.' It's profoundly simple and powerful, as is the message she wants to take to the world. 'We can choose life. We can choose to be victorious. We can choose to make a difference to the world, but we first need to choose to make a difference to who we are.'

It's exactly Maharishi's vision which drew me to Transcendental Meditation – to bring peace to the world through each of us finding peace within – and another beautiful alignment.

Victoria firmly believes she wouldn't be here if she hadn't believed in God. And that some of us are chosen to be part of the healing process for others. 'The darkness will try and take you out wherever it can,' she says pensively. 'Fighting for the light is a daily commitment. God will always know where we need to go well before we do, so we need to seek that guidance every day.'

She's come a long way from that day in hospital when she heard God's voice for the first time and it kick-started her quest to find greater meaning. She consulted spiritual advisers, took courses, read books and started praying in earnest. Though her 20s and early 30s she had many invitations to spark a deeper connection with God, stripping away another barrier to trust. 'It wasn't easy,' she admits. 'We go to God when things aren't great or we're in need. But it's only when we are on our knees in surrender, when we feel absolutely hopeless, that He can come in and turn our lives around. Because only then are we willing to listen.'

It takes me back to Charl's humble kitchen table. The circumstances couldn't be more different, but the likeness is undeniable. He was a man broken to the point of complete surrender and it was only then that he could learn to trust and accept God's plan and completely give into His will.

But while Charl is wedded to the doctrine of the Christian faith, for Victoria it's just the manifestation she knows. 'I don't get fixated on that stuff,' she says. 'It doesn't matter how you define it. God has many labels. As long as you find the path that works for you to make a difference in the world and fast track your connection.'

For a moment I reflect on the persona Victoria has created around God's energy – that of a man. Perhaps having a father figure she always longed for, comforts her in some way. After all, she's lost all the men in her life bar Noah. Or, perhaps, it's just the manifestation so many of us have come to adopt through Christian scripture.

As with many other religions, Abraham Hicks doesn't define God in physical form but rather speaks about being inside the vortex, representing when we are in alignment with Source energy. We find it when we are still, perhaps meditating or just contemplating. It's how we quiet the noise, the negativity. It's how we find inner peace and how we connect to truth.

'Your heart always knows the truth, because God is truth,' Victoria says. 'Our hearts connect us back home and the more we practise, the stronger the antennae.' Her connection is now so strong that before each meditation she visualises being filled with white light, a form of protection from unwanted energies. She finally has the direct dial she always craved and the signals couldn't be louder, like switching from analogue to fibre optics.

'Hello Coach is infused with the essence of God,' she says. 'We are merely a vessel for God's work to come to fruition and we all have a chance to fulfil our life purpose if we choose our calling.'

She believes God has a plan for all of us to reach enlightenment, that when we work out our gifts they become our message. It's not about creating global empires, we can be cleaners, teachers, yoga instructors, even just good listeners. 'Whatever path you choose, it's about owning it. It's about making it uniquely yours and trusting where you can be of service,' she says.

I think about my childhood nanny, Cathy Whiteman and her life of service, of all the impoverished around the world. How I for so long considered my life to have more meaning because of privilege. I feel ashamed of the notion, but equally elated to know that people like Cathy knew such deep fulfilment.

A gloom has set in over the bay, a bank of grey cloud shrouding the late afternoon sunshine. Victoria is hugging a knee against her chest, staring at the giant raindrops that start spattering the balcony table. Her poise is sphynx-like, her discourse soulful. I feel like it's intended only for me. But I know I'll be one of many and that's entirely the point.

'The moment we deviate from our soul's calling, we get disconnected,' she says. 'We disconnect from Source when we become human. Part of our experience is finding our way home again. It's a beautiful metamorphic journey of disconnection, curiosity, pain, trauma, suffering, surrender, acceptance, forgiveness, home. God will give us certain experiences to go though and if we're not clear on our purpose it can be a painful ride. My purpose has been clear for the last 30 years and life has been preparing me for this journey.'

It's what kept her going through all the setbacks. When she'd visited New York in 2012, she'd knocked on the door of every studio from NBC and Netflix to Endemol Shine and Oprah, trying to sell the idea of a TV show about women telling their inspiring stories. But the world wasn't ready, it wasn't sufficiently broken. They all asked 'Who is this woman and what language is she speaking? Talking about a spiritual revolution, the transformation of humanity?' She was a visionary before her time.

'Every step has helped me evolve into who I am,' she smiles. 'I don't have a cell in my body that has anger towards my father. He was part of my journey. Did I choose it? On a conscious level, no. On a spiritual level, on a soul level? Whatever it is, it's what we do in these moments that define who we are and the lives we live.'

Eyes wide open

In death, Victoria's mother became her greatest avatar. She is ever present, more so than her father. 'She's always leaving clear signs,' Victoria says. She tells me about the time when Noah was about to undergo surgery. Opening the wardrobe to dress for the hospital, a cashmere shawl that had belonged to her mother flew out, landing right at her feet. 'It was her way of saying I am here for you,' she smiles.

Like Victoria, Judith had an incredible connection with God. In the final days before her death, she could no longer cope with the pain. So Victoria moved her to a palliative care unit where she kept a bedside vigil.

'God was there,' Victoria says dead pan. 'I've seen His face many times now. There was such incredible beauty and peace in that room.' She describes her mother being locked in His gaze for three days until she finally passed. 'It was light and I could see a silhouette. She was so focused on where she needed to be, like she was in a trance. Like she knew she was going home. She looked so peaceful.'

Judith finally left her at four in the morning. Victoria drove down to Collaroy beach to watch the sunrise. As it crept over the horizon, she felt the presence of her mother behind her. 'She put her arms around me,' she says, her eyes welling up once more. 'She was showing me how she wanted me to remember her. She looked about 40, with beautiful flowing blonde hair. I always loved her hair. Then she went up into the clouds.'

As she wipes away the tears, she describes the clouds forming a heart shape around where her mother disappeared. After a long pause she reaches for her phone to show me the photo, perhaps in case I'm doubting her or because she just likes to remember. It's a clear morning but the sky is shrouded in grey, an orange band marking the horizon where the day awakes. Yet in the middle of the heavens is a patch of light impossibly white, shaped like a heart. 'You can't make stuff like this up,' she says.

Then, as I hand her back the phone I see it for the first time. 'Turn around,' I say smiling. She swings around in her chair to see the base of a rainbow towering up from the middle of the bay. It's as bright and bold as I've ever seen and never so close to the shore. The rain had stopped and the clouds were thinning. Now it's her gaze that is fixed, like she's speaking to her mother.

I sit in silence to give them a moment. When she finally reaches for the tissue pack, she tells me about when she had to clear out her mother's belongings. It was a couple of weeks after her death and Victoria hadn't yet felt her presence. So she asked her mother three questions out loud: 'Where are you? Who are you with? Are you okay?'

The following morning as she drove past a collection of boxes that she'd placed there the day before for council clean up, she paused. On top of the boxes lay three photographs. The first was of her mother in the garden, her favourite place. The second with Noah at his communion, in front of the cross, her arms wrapped around him. The third was with Victoria. She has no idea how the photos could have got there. Now they have pride of place on the mantelpiece in her home. 'God and mum is always here,' she says.

The late afternoon sun breaks through the clouds once more and lends a sheen to her blonde hair, giving the illusion of a halo. 'He is real. There's a whole universe out there we don't understand. It invigorates my faith every day. I cannot doubt it anymore.'

I reflect on her and my faith, our resolute belief in God. How for many people I know the very concept is like a red rag to a bull. I have good friends who call themselves agnostic, beautiful souls each one of them. But they are only non-believers in the image of God we have created as humans. Were you to ask them what they believe, it might be in the power of human connections or simply being a good person, being good parents. Doing to others as they would have done unto themselves. But these are the teachings of every religion or spiritual practice. Because they're the principles of love and God is love.

1 John 4:16 reads 'And so we know and rely on the love God has for us. God is love. Whoever lives in love lives in God and God in them.'

I think of my parents and their steady guiding hands. Did they know what they were doing raising four kids on the smell of an oily rag? Being pulled in all directions by their flock? No way. But they, too, never stopped trusting in God's plan.

And like Charl, Victoria also now understands it was never about her, it was always about the coaches, because she's completely devoid of ego. It's what comes from finding unconditional self-love after all these years, losing the judgements of who she thought she was or wasn't. 'I do love myself,' she says. 'But love for me is compassion. I feel the energy around me that opens my heart up to such an extent I feel unconditional love. Because I have surrendered as a vessel to do God's work. The rest is unimportant.'

It's another beautiful alignment with Charl's message: 'We are here to love and serve the Almighty God. Nothing else matters'.

oOo

Unbeknown to him, one of the many inspiring people along my journey has been American entrepreneur and author, Tim Ferriss. It was Victoria that introduced me to his podcasts. His sharing of his own story at the hands of a teenage boy's systematic abuse was compelling and he really endeared me to his work. It also helped me to appreciate just how prevalent it is and why it's so important for people like Tim and Victoria to tell their stories. Because it's only by shaking the stigma of abuse that people can be brave enough to start the long journey towards wholeness, even if it seems an impossible task.

If Victoria had it her way, she would free human existence of the very real and devastating effects of abuse that still permeate our society like a disease. 'Physical, mental, emotional or sexual abuse is far too rife,' she laments. 'And people are only now starting to speak up about it.' Victoria has a clear message. 'We are not the stories of our past and they can only define us if we let them,' she says in ultimate defiance. 'There is no shame in what happened to me. There are terrible atrocities perpetrated at the hands of cruel and wounded people every day. But if we are prepared to commit to and do the work on ourselves to heal our trauma, we ultimately have the chance to find forgiveness.'

Finding it in our hearts to forgive those who do us injustice must surely be our greatest challenge as human beings. I reflect on those that have ever caused harm to me, my friends or family. How naturally protective we all are, so quick and noble to gorge on fantasies of revenge. The key is letting go of ego, a concept that both scares and inspires me.

It scares me because we are so beholden to our ego that to shed it entirely is to lose part of who we are. In many ways we can't survive without it because it's been our entire sense of identity and our connection with this material world we have come to adore. For many of us it's our sole source of aspiration and perceived purpose. But it also inspires me because it's not real and its grip lightens a little more with every meditation.

oOo

The sun has set behind the national park headland that neatly conceals any signs of Sydney's CBD. Remnants of the moody clouds are edged in fiery orange, like a bright light shining from behind the darkness. Our session has finished and I watch Victoria's slim figure disappear through the doorway. The apartment is eerily empty, so I slide open the bi-fold doors to let in some air. The room is suddenly awash with sea salt and pine, the light southerly wind brushing against a row of Norfolk Island pine trees that decorate the skyline in front of my apartment.

But I'm too rapt by her story to appreciate the view, about how she's harnessed her trauma for the benefit of others and how fortunate the rest of us are to reap the rewards. How she simply couldn't have been ready or capable to do what she's doing had she not gone through all those years of hell. They were her words not mine, living in a place of sheer hopelessness, of all-consuming, desperate loneliness. But how the pain, heartache and suffering was a necessary part of her journey and how she's grateful to her father.

For the rest of her days Victoria sees herself as being a messenger. She's walked through fire, literally and figuratively. Now she's turning the mess into her message. She wants to give the world the tools to make sure no-one has to go through what she has. 'No-one should ever feel alone,' she said. 'No-one should ever feel that they don't have access to someone to help pull them out. I want to be part of people's ignition process to remember who they are. That's all my job is.' It's her rope ladder out of the abyss.

Hello Coach launched in April 2022 with 50 experienced coaches and a basket of blue-chip clients. Today it has over a thousand coaches and works with a multitude of large and small organisations. After a few false starts Victoria's dream has finally taken flight and she believes it will be successful exactly because its time has come. 'The world is ready to hear this now,' she said. 'It's in so much pain and in desperate need of healing.'

COVID-19 was a giant wake-up call especially for her corporate clients. It laid bare how much people are hurting, how much they need solutions to navigate the mental stress. It has spurred a realization that we have a responsibility to act with accountability, to pay attention to what's important, not just shovel lip service. And it's much bigger than a pesky virus. 'What we're dealing with now is a 50-year mental health epidemic and it's not going away,' she said. 'COVID-19 just helped us to open our eyes.'

More and more, corporates are recognising the need to focus on employee wholeness and not just wellness. It's what makes for genuinely sustainable business practices and improved productivity. Victoria's platform will provide the access point for so many people to begin asking the right questions, to raise their awareness of self and to focus on what's missing.

'We are responsible for the systematic collapse of our planet,' she said. 'Yet we continue running around in our corporate suits and fail to confront our true purpose. I have faith that this narrative is changing slowly - people are questioning who they are and are striving for lives that have more impact and purpose.' She's right and I can relate.

I work with great people on interesting clients, I'm constantly stimulated by situational challenges and enjoy the collegiate culture of my firm. But to what end do I keep greasing the wheels of the corporate treadmill? It's a question I ask myself with alarming regularity. The financial reward has always been a by-product of doing something I enjoy, something that keeps me inspired, develops my knowledge and expedites my growth. I have all of these things, yet the fact you're reading these pages is an instructive acknowledgement that it's not my true calling.

Over the years, my yearning to be more fulfilled has grown from a distant pulse to a thunderous foghorn. A yearning for something that feels intuitively right, something that will contribute to our purpose as a collective. Something that will help to take us closer to fulfilling Maharishi's dream of a world at peace with itself.

Like Victoria, I believe that this is all part of God's plan and that COVID-19 has been the catalyst to make us all think differently. It has forced us to test our values and beliefs, to question our relationships with one another and even question why we are here. We need to ask these existential questions, because they are the first step towards finding our purpose.

She is the first to acknowledge that the decisions we need to make to follow our true paths are often not easy. Like leaving our partners, subjecting our children to acrimonious divorce or giving up the security of our lucrative professions. But the signposts are always there, we just need to trust the messages we're receiving.

It's why Victoria's platform is exactly what the world needs, to help facilitate change at a planetary level. Corporations are run by people, after all. 'The pandemic has been a wake-up call to the collective and it's what we do at an individual level that will make the difference,' she said. It's about taking the best of the best and giving them the platform to create a divine connection and to help people realise that they matter. That everyone has the ability to live a victorious life no matter their circumstances.

oOo

One of Victoria's most remarkable features is the clarity of her eyes. It was the first thing I noticed about her when we met. I asked whether she wore special contact lenses but she just shook her head and looked at me quizzically. It would only be much further along my own journey that I'd realise the clarity of one's eyes has nothing to do with the outside. They are literally the windows into our souls and hers is as pure as the driven snow. It's why the time I spend in her company is so precious, like eavesdropping on her direct-dial with God.

Like Charl, it was only in sheer worthlessness that she could come to a point of surrender and like Charl, her life is no longer her own but rather one of example. It takes a remarkable human to be disconnected for so long and still find a way out of the abyss and to break the choking cycle of abuse. There was a sheer determination in saving herself from her father's toxic shadow, in peeling back the layers of her past and finding the self-love she needed to do God's work. Privilege plays no part in our preservation.

Coming through it all, then, I can only imagine the pain that losing her mother must have caused, her ultimate bastion and confidante stolen from her in a whisk. I wonder, had her mother had the same self-knowledge and determination could she have saved herself? The irony is it was Victoria who lived with all those years of disease and her life could just as easily have been one of attrition.

I get the sense though, that even in those darkest hours she felt a responsibility to find herself and live out her true potential. There is nothing clever in martyring ourselves and is that not a far truer reflection of God's love? The sad thing is that for most of us, we don't make the time. As Victoria points out there is no instant gratification, we all have to do the work. Life's no easy ride and we will always suffer injustices.

But we can choose to stay the course and when we hear the knock, we can be courageous enough to answer. Because we are worth it and we all have the same power to bring about meaningful change. Surely, then, when the time comes is it not also incumbent on us to make the right choices?

13
Jude's calling

When Jude-Martin Etuka walked through the black wrought-iron gates of Blackfriars Hall that crisp Autumn morning an elation took hold, the sort of which he had never known. Through its sandstone archway the sky looked especially blue, like the iris in bloom.

Clutching the black and white habit under his arm he stepped briskly onto the Oxford pavement and didn't look back. The squeak of his new leather brogues, in particular, made him smile. Of all the rituals that had defined his last seven years, crossing the monastery courtyard in open sandals for their dawn service was one he surely wouldn't miss.

For a moment he stopped, spellbound by the idea he could go wherever he pleased. Exhaling deeply, he watched the cloud of condensation clear before him. St Giles' Street was decidedly still. Even the procession of oak trees stood undisturbed, painting the smattering of parked cars and padlocked bicycles in shadow. It was a definitive moment in time.

He ran his hand along the church's rough sandstone wall, a final gesture of gratitude. Then reaching the corner, he glanced up at the stained-glass windows he'd spent so many hours admiring from the other side, their intricate portraits backlit by the outside world. From where he stood, they weren't nearly as splendid.

He crossed the road, then quickened his pace until he was beneath the signboard of a giant eagle carrying a baby in swaddling. Cupping his hands over one of the small windowpanes, he peered inside the empty public house. It was not as he'd imagined.

A pleasant jingle rang overhead as he stepped through the Tudor-era door. Despite a low ceiling the air was fresh, with a hint of holly. He breathed into his hands for warmth.

'Morning, guv'nor,' said a gentleman appearing around the corner of the rectangular bar. Wispy blonde hair and cherry cheeks gave the impression of a man who might spend a lot of time there. 'Never too early for a sharp'ner, what's your flavour?' He whipped the chequered dishcloth from his shoulder and picked up a glass to polish.

'Yes, it is a good morning,' Jude-Martin said in refined English, the product of the Chelsea childhood he'd enjoyed before he'd returned to his Nigerian homeland. 'A pint of Guinness, good sir. I would really love a pint of Guinness.'

'Comin' right up.' Deftly hanging the glass on a hook above the dark wooden bar, the proprietor reached for a taller one bearing the infamous harp emblem. Then in a smooth, stylish motion he eased the ivory tap toward him.

Jude-Martin followed the swirling cloud settling into distinctive black and white lines, like the habit he now set down on a small table to his right. He watched as his dark features warped in the polished brass bar handle as he reached for his beer.

'You one of 'em brothers?' the proprietor asked half surprised.

'I was, yes,' Jude-Martin smiled. 'Until this very morning.'

He ran his tongue over a creamy upper lip and set the beer back down. A warm flush sent his neck hair to attention. Never had he felt more alive, yet imbued with this newfound sense of freedom there was an uncomfortable bewilderment.

Since entering the monastery at 17 he'd spared no thought for the day's agenda, each minute accounted for from the bell's first chime. It was one of the ways he and the brothers stayed present in their pursuits. Now, the idea of making choices carried a strange burden of responsibility.

He glanced at the ornate, oversized clock in an adjacent room, out of place among the otherwise modest fittings. 10.50 am. They would just be settling into silent meditation. He closed his eyes momentarily, contemplating the inner bliss.

'Where you headed?' Jude-Martin did all he could not to flinch at the disturbance.

'London,' he said. 'I'm catching the 11.30 to Paddington to see my brother.' The idea of the train ride alone was a thrill. Jude-Martin averted the barman's eyes as he recalled the phone conversation with his parents – his father's blatant disappointment, his mother's poorly masked sadness. How long would it be before he could face them?

'You got time for another then,' the barman clucked as if pleased with himself. 'Tell you what, you can have two for a tenner, being such a special day an' all.'

Suddenly embarrassed, Jude-Martin reached for his habit and unrolled it on the table. He retrieved a brown leather pouch from between his toothbrush and razor. It was a parting gift from the Order to see him on his way.

As he held out a crisp ten-pound note, the vows he'd sworn under the domed roof of Blackfriars Hall reverberated through his mind. His unwavering commitment to a life of poverty, chastity and obedience. How long would it be until the shame began to fade?

A bitter aftertaste ran down his throat. Perhaps a second beer was just what he needed.

oOo

I met Jude-Martin Etuka, or Jude as his friends call him, in Cape Town shortly after the turn of the millennium. A friend of my brother's, I recall being decidedly shocked when a crisp British accent emanated from the beaming black man with tied-back dreadlocks. Despite appearances, there was something quite regal in his demeanour, like he owned the space around him.

Jude goes by his baptismal Catholic name. Onuora, his African name, means 'mouth of the people' – given his yearning to heal the world it seems entirely appropriate. It is this yearning that has brought us together all these years later.

After fleeting re-acquaintanceships in London, we reconnected in earnest during my brother's last visit to Sydney. Jude had beaten me here by a handful of years and it was over dinner at Customs House that I first came to know Jude-Martin Etuka, monk of the Dominican Order.

Sitting outside on a warm spring evening, a homeless woman approached our table from behind me. Jude gave off no hint of apprehension, just a warm and welcoming smile.

'G'day fellas. Spare a bit of change for a bed at the Salvos?' she said. Of aboriginal heritage, she cut a diminutive figure beside the high table, aided by a subtle hunchback.

'I recognise you,' Jude chuckled waving his finger. 'I've met you before.' Evidently taken aback, the woman squinted in his direction.

'I met a lotta fellas,' she rasped, revealing a near-full set of yellow teeth. 'But none too many like you.' Choosing our table had evidently been no accident.

'Yes, yes, yes,' Jude said. 'I have met you, I'm sure of it. Down at Central Station.'

'Oh yeah, yeah,' she stammered, absent of any hint of recognition. 'Central, yeah. I been there few times.'

'We spoke, remember? You told me about needing to go to hospital and I gave you some money.'

'Aah, yeah I know, I know.' She was putting it on thick now, spurred on by the knowledge of prior success. 'Central, yeah, yeah. Everything much better now,' she said rubbing her lower back.

'That's good to hear.'

Jude reached into his folded jacket on the stool beside him. Opening his wallet, he handed her a ten dollar note.

'Now you look after yourself,' he said as she slid the note between layers of soiled clothing. 'I'm sure I'll be seeing you again.'

'God bless you, brother,' she said and shuffled quickly away, as if he might change his mind. She may well have muttered the words again but was already half-way across the promenade towards Circular Quay.

Jude turned back to face me, still beaming. Dark-rimmed spectacles accentuated his bright brown eyes, his smooth bald head offering no hint of his 49 years. Then he leaned forward. 'Now where were we?' Once again he is fully present. It's just him and me, like I'm the only person on earth.

'Ah yes, you were asking about Nigeria.' Before he begins regaling me with stories of his adolescent years, he nods a few times in silence. Reminiscing, like he's back in Lagos, taking in the smell of deep-fried plantain and ever-present dust from the untarred street in front of the family apartment, sidestepping the heavy-laden hawkers. It's been nearly 30 years since he left and he makes no bones about a deep longing to return.

Growing up in Chelsea, one of London's most prestigious boroughs, Jude was eight when he and his brothers moved to Nigeria. Touted as a long-overdue family holiday to the homeland, it was only on touching down in its capital that their father dropped the bombshell. It was to be their new home.

To a young boy it was an especially foreign world, a complete social and cultural upheaval where staples like water and electricity were luxuries. He quickly learned what it was like not to have and to appreciate all that we take for granted, while intermittent trips back to see his friends would reinforce the juxtaposition. It was a perfect training ground for the monastery.

What made relocating to Lagos all the more curious was the successful career his father had forged as a black barrister. London in the 1950s saw the Notting Hill race riots, the emergence of far-right groups like the White Defence League and 'No blacks, no dogs, no Irish' signs brandished over would-be rental properties. As a young boy, Jude struggled to come to terms with it all, as did I in apartheid South Africa.

Many Nigerians had made their way to London, encouraged to go and study under their colonial masters. Among them was a bright law student named Raphael Etuka, who with his young bride Christina, set off to forge a new life. He completed his law degree at Kings College, then built a private practice with 20 years of toil and dogged determination.

Raphael was a man of staunch principle. He put every last penny into educating his four boys, even if it meant foregoing food. It was with no small amount of trepidation, therefore, that he had plucked his children from their first-class British schools: the native call of Africa had become too strong to ignore.

In hindsight, it was the greatest gift he could have given Jude and his three brothers. They were to start afresh, to drink from the chalice of hard knocks and given his time again Jude wouldn't change a thing. 'It's what made me the man I am today,' he says. 'It really opened my eyes, allowed me to see and understand the world for the first time.' There is a deep sincerity about him that he wears like a badge of honour. I find myself hanging on his every word. 'And it's ultimately why I chose to pursue a life of service to God.'

As devout Christians, when they re-settled in Lagos, Raphael and Christina were quick to establish themselves as active members of St Dominic's Catholic Church. They regularly attended services, conducted Sunday readings and donated handsomely to its coffers. Such was their standing in the community that it was not infrequent for the priest of St Dominic's to join the Etukas for supper and evening prayer.

It was therefore with God ever-present in their lives that Jude developed a natural interest in all things spiritual, strongly encouraged by his mother. She, too, had been raised by staunch Catholics, while being blessed with the voice of an angel meant she was steeped in Christian music from a young age. It would very nearly lead to her enrolment as a nun, for she was also deeply spiritual with a gift for knowing things about people she'd never even met. She chose instead to teach music and to have a family of her own. It's why Jude's path to the monastic order was paved with her blessings.

But ultimately it was the ebullient monks who preached from atop St Dominic's altar that would inspire him to don their robes. The spectacle of thousands of parishioners spilling from its pews onto rolling lawns outside, hands raised aloft, lifting the roof in praise.

'It was more a natural progression than a calling,' Jude says in answer to my question. It's prompted by the conversations I had with my father about why he became a priest, although the differences to joining the Catholic Dominicans are not lost on me.

'I always had a strong relationship with God and my parents played no small part in that,' Jude says. 'But I also felt a deep sense that something was missing, that there was something which needed to be fulfilled.' The answers, he believed, lay within the walls of the monastery in Ibadan, some 130 kilometres northeast of Lagos. He was to train there as a monk, taking their sacred vows of poverty, chastity and obedience.

Naturally it was not a decision he took lightly. As a healthy young man he was not immune to the temptations of the flesh and what he found even more daunting was the need to remove himself entirely from society, to forego all possessions and live in complete community. But when special dispensation came from Rome for him to join the Order at 17, Raphael and Christina Etuka could not have been more delighted. Jude's fate was sealed.

Brothers in arms

In 1216, Castilian priest Dominic de Guzmán started a religious order of the Catholic Church now known as the Dominicans. It is also said to have derived its name from the Latin *domini canes*, meaning 'dogs of the Lord', in mock-derision of the friars who barked Christ's gospel and guarded against deviation from the path to salvation.

The Dominican Order is based on a spiritual and intellectual quest to know and understand God and a simple premise that belief in God and in the Christian faith is both rational and completes the fundamental human desire for truth and righteousness.

Its friars follow a life of meditation, silence, fasting and relentless study of theology and philosophy, spirituality and the lives of mystics and saints. It is for this reason that the Dominicans embedded themselves in universities around the world, engaging with their ideas and ideals. For more than 800 years the Order has been actively involved in theological education, Oxford's Blackfriars Hall in particular, producing several well-known preachers and philosophers, not all Christian.

It was there that Jude found himself on his eventual return from Nigeria some 13 years later, seeing out the rest of his time in the Dominican brotherhood. While the Dominican

University at Ibadan had provided an unmatched richness in spiritual fulfilment, it was within the smaller but more keenly-minded fraternity at Blackfriars Hall that he would immerse himself in daily philosophical deliberations.

From the outset they were taught a universal approach to God. As a secular university, Oxford's lecturers included former Catholic priests, Buddhists and Atheist alike. They studied Christian ecumenism, a holistic approach to Christianity that promotes unity across all denominations and in their philosophy lectures they'd tear the Christian faith apart, testing its boundaries to breaking point. For some of the students it was all too much.

'They felt theologically violated and had to leave,' Jude says earnestly. 'They just couldn't deal with their faith being turned inside out like that.'

It was designed to rid students of all their preconceptions and start afresh, to strip them back to nothing and eliminate the noise, to learn just to be. It is here that Jude began to find the answers he was looking for and where his journey of enlightenment began.

It was a journey that started each day with the five o'clock bell and culminated in solitude. In between, however, from morning mass to evening dinner the brothers were always together – meditating, praying, studying and worshipping in community. On occasion, when it was permitted to play team sports, they played together and on feast days and birthdays they celebrated together. The brothers were his family, united.

Reformed businessman Brother Godwin – 25 years Jude's elder – was something of a father figure to him; Brother Alfonsis, with his infinite energy and focus, could be found praying in his room at almost any hour and seldom joined them at mealtimes so prone was he to fasting; and the spiritually-gifted Brother Augustin, who'd counsel his widely-travelled visitors before they even had time to bear their souls.

Jude admired and adored his brothers. It was among them that he found his spiritual groove and developed a deep love of intellectual pursuits and of silence and introspection.

Unlike Diocesan priests like my father, the friars had little interaction with the outside world. No-one left the monastery walls unless under exceptional circumstances and with special dispensation from the Prior. Their learnings and experiences were shared only with one another.

'Contemplate and give unto others the fruits of your contemplation,' Jude says thoughtfully. It had been ingrained in them from day one. 'The meditation and silence meant nothing unless we could share their beauty with our brothers. The Lord says you must love one another as you love yourself.'

After seven years in the monastery, ordination into the priesthood loomed. Jude had reached a crossroads and sharing these learnings with his brothers alone had left something unfulfilled in the young monk from Chelsea. He couldn't place it, but it had grown louder, like the nagging of a petulant child. It was an inner calling that he'd got what he needed and that it was time to spread his celestial wings.

So, with the Prior's blessing he went into silent retreat at the Jesuit Monastic Order in Heathrow, praying for two weeks for God to guide his decision and that he may find peace with it.

It was with a grave heart that Jude returned to Blackfriars Hall in Autumn 1995 to break the news to his brothers. In the end, it was their unwavering support and empathy that put a spring in his step that crisp morning. And as his brogues clip-clopped along St Giles' Street towards the Eagle and Child, his world was shucked open like an oyster.

oOo

Jude's last call had not been a pleasant one: not even affording his son the opportunity to explain himself, it would be six months before Raphael Etuka spoke to him again. As a devout man of God, it was a nail in the heart. Forgiveness for his son, as it turned out, would take considerably longer.

So it was to Paul, his brother, that Jude turned when he left the Order and in whose embrace he found solace on a bustling Paddington station platform.

As much as he loved all of his brothers, Paul was his favourite. Jude was closer in age to Mike and Chuks, but always had a particular affinity with Paul. 'He was such a humble man,' Jude says with a hint of melancholy. 'So down-to-earth, so happy-go-lucky. There was nothing we didn't share.' He pauses, looking at his interlocked fingers resting on the table. 'He was such a great listener. We used to talk on the phone for hours, then I'd realise he'd hardly said a word.'

It was from Paul's empathy that Jude had drawn so much strength. It's why his death had been such a hammer blow.

Suffering from kidney pain, he'd gone to hospital for routine tests. But it was his high blood pressure that concerned the doctors, so they put a stent in his aorta. Only it proceeded to leak, causing endocarditis. They did all that they could to save him, but in the end, he died still complaining of pain in his kidneys. He was 51-years-old.

Jude had long left London and hadn't seen his eldest brother for five years. It was during one of their weekly conversations, though, that he realised he needed to fly home. Paul was about to go in for his final procedure and ironically, it was his calm demeanour that concerned Jude the most. 'Paul had been in such a panic before,' Jude says. 'It was like he'd made peace with his demons and that he knew he wasn't going to make it off the operating table.'

Jude booked the first available ticket from Sydney to London, but on checking his phone at the Abu Dhabi stopover, his heart sank. Returning one of the five missed calls from his mother, he knew he was too late: that the conversation with Paul had been his last.

The second leg into London Heathrow was the loneliest few hours of Jude's life. And on arrival he had to summon the will to pick up the pieces of his shattered family.

Like all of them, Paul had been a very active member of the Catholic Church. These things simply didn't happen to such God-loving people. In Nigerian custom you didn't bury your children, they buried you.

It would prove too much for 75-year-old Christina to manage, both physically and mentally. She suffered a stroke, losing partial movement of her left arm. She'd been at Paul's side every day in hospital and when he passed, part of her soul went with him.

Again, I'm at Mike's bedside in Tygerberg Hospital, watching the fluids run down tubes in his arms and throat, telling him how much I love him. It is surely only in losing such good people that we can really grow; that we can learn about pain and sorrow. Learn how to heal and pass on that wisdom to those who need it.

For Jude, as devastating as Paul's death was, he's the first to acknowledge it is just part of life's rich tapestry; all part of God's plan. And that everything works out for the greater good. 'Even in his death, Paul was a uniting force for the family,' Jude says. 'It brought us closer together. Of course, we always loved each other, but no-one ever said the words. Now we say it in every conversation.' Even the stoic Raphael Etuka tells his boys he loves them each time they speak, just in case it's the last. There is no more holding back emotion in the Etuka family.

Today, his parents have nothing but support for Jude's decision to leave the Order. He finally has the acceptance he desperately craved, but it's not just because of Paul's death. Under Nigerian custom, as the main breadwinner, it is now incumbent on Jude to support the whole family. It's why he's so determined to make a success of his coaching business and is well on the way to realising his dream, while supporting his own young family and completing his PhD so he can pass on his learnings, only this time to hundreds of students at a time.

Ironically, it's Jude that wears the cloak of responsibility because Mike, now the oldest, traded a career in law enforcement for the priesthood – not in the Dominican Order, but as a diocesan Catholic priest. And when Mike calls, it's Jude who now does the listening.

In time, he will hand the mantle to Chuks, the youngest and six years Jude's junior. Before Chuks' arrival their mother had miscarried while expecting her first daughter. It's what made the loss all the more devastating. Short for Chukwuemeka, Chuks means 'God did great deeds'. It seems fitting that he alone chose to keep his Nigerian name. And answers why, when Jude's wife Romina fell pregnant, Jude so desperately wanted a girl.

Keeping it a surprise until the birth, they named their daughter Raphaella, after his father.

Avowed intentions

After leaving Blackfriars Hall that Autumn morning, Jude enrolled at Northwick Park Hospital in Harrow as an unregistered trainee nurse. He took issue with the way psychiatric patients were treated, so he signed up for the mental health ward. Constantly pacified or sedated with drugs, there was no pathway for them to heal and so to treat people who couldn't manage themselves internally seemed an appropriate transition for him at the time.

They suffered delusions of grandeur and were slaves to the voices in their heads. He felt he could help by applying his experience as a monk, giving them the tools to manage their mindset and to help them to step outside their mind, to realise they weren't beholden to it.

He loved the people there and threw himself headlong into the work, doing as many shifts as he could to fund the rest of his master's degree at Oxford. Finishing the night shift at six in the morning, he'd steel home to his shared London digs for two hours sleep, then race back up to Oxford in his banged-up Fiat Punto in time for morning lectures.

When occasion permitted, he'd attend Oxford student parties to maintain a semblance of his own sanity. You could always find him in the corner with a pint glass of cheap red wine, sharing the fruits of his contemplation with anyone inclined to listen.

Jude was perpetually skint, so after two years and his master's finally under his belt, he took a second job in HR recruitment at Nestor Healthcare in London. Instead of driving up to Oxford for lectures, after his night shift at the hospital, he'd change into a suit in the back seat and drive the 21 kilometres straight into central London to recruit mental health doctors and nurses for his second job. Only then would he go home, scraping whatever sleep he could before doing it all over again.

In between it all he lectured MBA students at Middlesex University where he completed a second master's, this time in human resources and still found time to go off the rails. He was a free man, after all – of chastity and obedience, too. He immersed himself in London's burgeoning nightlife and festival scene, where we'd had most of our prior encounters. It's why when I finally got to know Jude, brother of the Dominican Order that evening at Customs House, it had been so enlightening.

But even in those "wayward years" as he describes them, he never lost touch with himself. The heartbeat was always there and when he came back to meditation it was like he'd never left. 25 years since walking out of Blackfriars Hall he still considers himself one of the brothers. 'You can take the monk out of the monastery, but you can never take the monastery out of the monk,' he laughs.

Nowadays when he meditates, he still sees himself in the black and white habit. He feels it on his body. And while he has lost touch with Godwin, Alfonsis and Augustin, they remain a constant source of inspiration. 'Whenever I think it's all getting too much, I think of Alfonsis praying and fasting at three in the morning,' Jude laughs. 'Or when I'm struggling to find the right answers, I ask myself what Augustin would say.' The recollections stir something in him, like he's still connected with them in some parallel realm.

The vows they took, too, remain deeply ingrained in him and it's only since departing the Order that he's come to truly appreciate their purpose.

Through the vow of poverty, he's learned to disassociate from worldly things. To be *in* the world, but not be *of* the world. Like anyone he enjoys the finer things in life but he has no attachment to anything physical. He uses 'dis-identification' as a spiritual term, a deeper knowing that everything is transitory. 'I lived that when Paul died,' he says. 'I saw him transition from the physical world to where he is now. I still speak to him all the time.'

It reminds me of Victoria's parents, how they now play such a constructive part in her life, her mother especially. And how that allows her to feel close to them.

Now a happily married man, through the vow of chastity Jude learned to control his desires, to maintain self-discipline. 'People get lost in the whirlwind of desire,' he says. 'The ability to manage our impulses is possibly the greatest challenge we face as humans.' He's quoting renowned author Daniel Goleman. And we can surely all relate to that, the world we live in is designed to stimulate impulse at every turn. To have us obsess over the next shiny thing and lose touch with what's real.

Finally, obedience. The 'vow of all vows', as Jude calls it. As brothers they'd obeyed the Prior without question, understanding his decisions to be borne of the Holy Spirit for the greater good of the community. But beyond the monastery walls its application was so much more significant. 'It's in the acceptance of a higher power that what we are being asked to do is the right path for us,' Jude says. 'It's about trust and giving ourselves to non-resistance, to the flow of life.' It's Abraham Hicks's vortex.

Today he applies these vows to all aspects of his coaching, including in the corporate sphere. 'Companies tend to put life in a box,' he says, 'to rid it of spontaneity. My job is to break the restrictive frameworks and help build in flexibility. Knowing that flow will achieve the best outcome opens up so many possibilities.'

He tells me about a senior engineer who broke down in front of his entire executive team. Jude had started the session by sitting in silence for three minutes. It's a technique he uses to connect with those he's trying to help. To disarm them and win their steadfast attention. The silence had taken the man back to a place of recent trauma and into its vacuum flooded his suppressed emotions, surprising him as much as his colleagues. But it engendered a most natural and powerful healing process.

With Jude, this is the rule and not the exception. It's no wonder he's called the master of silence. It's just one of the many ways that he reaches people.

In 2021 I attended a five-day silent Vipassana retreat, a Buddhist term meaning 'insight'. The only opportunity to speak was in open sharing sessions with a mindfulness teacher, usually up on stage while the rest of the group listened. It could be to ask a question or share an experience, but what amazed me was how vulnerable so many people were prepared to be in front of strangers. To open up about their pain and suffering. It was immensely powerful precisely because it was real. We could all identify with their situations in our own way.

But it's not just his coaching to which Jude still applies the vows of the Order. He channels them to strengthen his alignment with God, applying the theological texts he devoted his youth to in everyday life. 'You get to this *lived* experience through your meditation and contemplation,' Jude says. 'Through thinking, feeling and behaving in all aspects of these vows.'

It's an understanding and appreciation that continues to grow, the founding teachings of the monastic order being an intense preparation for everything he's doing today. It's sharing this with others that gives him such unbridled joy and daily realisations of why he had the "calling to leave".

The answers he sought when leaving Blackfriars Hall that day would be a long time coming, but when they did it was like the scales falling from his eyes.

oOo

After those early years of toil Jude landed a human resources job with Transport for London, then consulting firm Capita. He could finally appreciate a full night's sleep and traded the back seat of his car for a walk-in wardrobe. He started his own HR consulting practice, then he moved to Australia with Romina and Raphaella. He chased the sun, as I had, sought to reconnect with Mother Nature. But something fundamental still eluded him.

It was then that a friend introduced him to neurolinguistic programming, or NLP. He knew instantly it was what he'd been searching for. He could finally harmonise his studies and his time as a monk. He finally understood that the vows are designed to manage our bodies, minds and our emotions so that we can reach the summit of our spiritual selves.

The fundamental premise of NLP is the relationship between thinking, feeling and behaving. It borrows from the tenets of philosophy and theology, tying everything from his past in a shiny red ribbon, complete with a gift pack of tools on how to apply them.

It was then that he picked up a copy of *The Power of Now* by Eckhart Tolle. It reinforced this alignment between NLP and his teachings in theology and philosophy and drove home the fundamental idea that we are not our minds.

'It's still the thing that gets most people's attention,' Jude laughs. 'A lot of the time it's met with enormous relief. As people we are hallucinating all the time. The only difference between us and those suffering from psychosis is that *they* don't know when they're hallucinating.'

He sees now that his long and often taxing journey was no accident. His seven years in silence and meditation, liberally enriched by the Holy Spirit at St Dominic's and the fierce intellect of Blackfriars Hall. His time as a mental health nurse, his training in coaching and NLP, Paul's death and the blessings of his own family.

It's what makes him so proficient in helping people to step outside their minds to observe them from a spiritual place, a place where they can be one with God. Where all religious and spiritual preconceptions, east and west, dissolve into the giant melting pot of unity.

It's the same unified field into which I dip my toe each time I practise Transcendental Meditation. It's the stillness in those who practise Buddhist Mindfulness. It's the solemn prayer and contemplation of Charl and my father. It's the silent introspection of the brothers of the Dominican Order.

'Religion is just a concept created by our minds,' Jude says. 'It's only when we step out of our minds that we realise there's no difference. Catholicism has a universal approach to God. Some particular dogmas of the Catholic faith may not be recognised by others, but they all point to the same thing.'

It's beautifully harmonious. What I have come to appreciate more than anything is that enlightenment is not some miraculous realisation we wake up to one morning. It's something we achieve every day on our long and winding spiritual journeys, each unique, like snowflakes. Just as children on opposite ends of the world raised with conflicting influences can end up with the same morals and belief structures, it doesn't matter how we get there, just that we do.

There will naturally always be those who are at the outer extremes, for whom this ideal is too difficult to accept. It's these extremists that stigmatise otherwise wholesome religious practices precisely because their specific belief structures are too deeply ingrained. They are too closely aligned with their identity, they fear by letting go they will lose themselves entirely. But it's this very mindset that Jude and his brothers so ably broke down and put back together in Blackfriars Hall. No king's horses, no king's men.

'There will always be polarities,' Jude says. 'But we sit in the middle. We get to see both ends of it and realise there is no pole at all. It is just unity. Whether you're Christian, Jewish, Muslim or Hindu, it's all about your own journey of enlightenment. And it's only when you progress far enough up the spiritual ladder that these differences and characterisations dissipate.'

Like climbing my beanstalk and sticking my head through the clouds for the first time, seeing the world anew.

Our evening is drawing to a natural close. For a moment I shut my eyes and picture myself sitting alone in the pews of Blackfriars Hall, while Jude stands on the altar in his flowing black and white habit, like the monks of St Dominic's of Lagos. I tune in to the richness of his voice. When I open my eyes, a soft yellow light from the Customs House doorway forms a halo around his smooth dark head.

'When we spoke as brothers we called it God, Jesus, the Holy Spirit,' he says with unwavering passion. 'In eastern terminology they talk about 'being', 'source' or 'otherness'. These are just language differences that are contextual to a particular following. Even within Buddhism there are different approaches. But the language used does not epitomise that towards which it points. It will always be insufficient attempting to point to the ineffable.'

He pauses, as if receiving one final message that he needs to convey. 'We are all seeking a closeness to God. And the Glory of God is man fully alive.'

oOo

As he puts the finishing touches to his PhD, Jude is hopeful that his brothers at Blackfriars Hall will one day get to read the fruits of his years of contemplation. It's titled *How emotional intelligence and NLP can influence transformational leadership*. It uncovers the process of how successful emotionally intelligent leaders got to where they are, how they attained their level of genius and learned to stay there. How they see, hear and feel, so it can serve as a model to others who seek to lead by example and inspire them to open up to life's natural flow.

He longs to return to the lectern, this time as a professor. In some ways it will complete the circle, finish what he started. And finally put to rest the disparaging words of those Oxford academics who told him he wasn't good enough. Not out of ego, but out of a desire to prove to himself that he is worthy.

I asked him who it was that told him that. Instead of naming names, he just smiles and points out the NLP technique I've just inadvertently used. To make him go inside and open up to fully being himself.

What he looks forward to most, though, is what the future holds along his continual journey. The beauty of the unknown. Like me, Charl and Victoria, he feels about ready to kick off life's second half. To have God use him to heal those that need it most. To help elevate human consciousness, one at a time.

'It's not about changing the masses,' he smiles as we embrace in front of Customs House. The large forecourt leading to its iconic façade is bathed in the light of a full moon. 'It's about helping individuals seek inward change.'

Maharishi's vision seems a fitting last word.

Above all else, it is Jude's humility that gives him such a powerful presence. And I have no doubt that it will, indeed, be the masses that are enriched by it.

I stand and watch him disappear around the corner of Circular Quay station on his way to catch a train home. But not before stopping to give a homeless man another note from his wallet and have a quick chat.

oOo

Jude is a beautiful man. The world is full of beautiful people and we can never be so fortunate to meet them all. But those that we do, we must surely cherish.

The fruits of his years of contemplation have been the final nails in my coffin of conviction. Within it lie the answers to all of our existential questions, like a Rubik's Cube smashed apart and systematically put back together, one twist at a time. I can bury it now with a full heart and a complete understanding of the power that lies within us all and of my father's calling. On its simple plaque are words of gratitude to my parents, Cathy, Mike, Charl, Victoria and Jude, the monk of the Dominican Order.

For those of us that choose to know God, how can we not also acknowledge and celebrate the fact that we are all united in the love of the same God? Otherwise, are we not denying ourselves our very purpose – to grow together as a collective consciousness? My hope is that others, too, come to discover that it is only in this way that we can make a difference as humanity and that the longer we limp forward in blinkered denial, the longer we rob ourselves of the chance to initiate meaningful change.

PART III

REVELATIONS

14

... Like son: confronting self

Shortly after Easter 2020, Dad sent me a recording of his sermon. He'd been invited to preach at his former Pinelands parish, but owing to lockdown it would be through an online text messaging and video service that the congregants of St. Stephen's would receive God's word that day, from the comfort of their armchairs.

He preaches of the beginnings of the church under threat of Roman persecution, not least at the hands of Saul, who would in time take the name of Paul and become one of Jesus's most fervent apostles. Christian deacon Stephen had just been stoned to death under his authority, the church's first martyr. It's an historic event well-known to St Stephen's parishioners.

He then talks of the apostles' courage, preaching in defiance of the authorities even in Jerusalem itself. How their subjects scattered like seeds, spreading God's word beyond the Holy City and how the roots of the Church began to take hold, nourished by the blood of martyrs like Stephen. Then he brings it back to the turmoil of the present world, with a clear message – even when things are at their darkest, in knowing God there is always life and there is always hope.

I am suddenly thrust back to the front line of the struggle, watching Dad march down Queen Victoria Street from St George's Cathedral, arm in arm with his brothers and sisters of every denomination. I hear them chant *'Apartheid won't live forever but we will – bring back free will!'* as the Special Branch water cannons swivel at the ready.

I'm reminded of his lay ministry programme, empowering so many to scatter like seeds and spread the Holy word, the churches he built and the spiritual bonfires he lit with the torch of the renewal movement. In my travels I have visited more magnificent churches and cathedrals than I could possibly recall, their ornate and intricate structures as marvellous as they are mesmerising. But never have I witnessed the power of the Holy Spirit more than in the simple pews of St Aidan's in Lansdowne, songs of praise lifting the roof of the hexagonal church to the upbeat three-piece corner band.

I look up at my father, one hand aloft and the other rattling a tambourine against his flowing white cassock. Beside me, Cathy is singing, eyes closed, lost in praise. I squeeze my mother's hand on the other side. She breaks from song to look down at me and smile. I am surrounded by love. That is how I grew up.

Forget about the isolation of living in Afrikaner country, the bedwetting and troubled dreams or the impoverished surrounds in which we spent our childhood, I was carried through it all in the hands of these, my spiritual guides. They were my role models. They instilled in me a moral compass that ensured I would never stray too far from my chosen path and have a desire to know God as they did, in their hearts.

For so much of my life I envied my father because his calling came so early, his purpose rolled out before him like a red carpet. But with it came a burden of expectation. On so many levels the life he chose has been challenging and confronting, both as a man and as a man of God. It's a course that has tested his principles, convictions and ultimately his faith. Learning to trust in God to guide him at every turn, to provide for him when he felt most helpless and to nourish him in his darkest hours.

But the rewards have been immeasurable. The riches he has received from dedicating his life to God are those that most of us dedicate our lives to seeking out – living a fulfilling, peaceful and joyful life, one that is immersed in love.

I always believed that I knew my father the man. Our childhoods saw us share a fundamental need to break free from our cages of conformity and forge our own identities. We were both rebels looking for our cause. And I was as steadfast in my determination not to follow in his footsteps as he was to not follow in his father's, for the very reason we now share his greatest regret. The inability to provide materially for us was his cross to bear, knowing this is my own to carry.

But while we are fundamentally the same, our journeys took us on very different generational paths. I needed to go and see the world, to immerse myself in its kaleidoscope of cultures and socio-economic settings, to put my perceived inadequacies into perspective and first and foremost to learn about myself.

Travel has had singularly the greatest influence on my life – experiencing new cultures, places, friendships and faces. They all teach you something, inspire you in some way. They crack open the boundaries of conformity and rip off your blinkers, so you see the world altogether differently. When you immerse yourself in humanity it's impossible not to fall in love with its kinks and curves; there is no greater paragon for our connectedness than accepting kindness from a stranger.

Having finally broken free from the confines of my upbringing and my parents' shadow, I had an insatiable and often reckless need to test what was possible, perhaps much like Dad did when he left home. Without the safety net my actions had far more severe consequences, yet I was never more cavalier. Any one of the tequila binges or run-ins with the Mexican authorities might have seen me buried in a dusty back alley or fed to the inhabitants of a remote island prison. Yet these were lessons I seemed to need to learn time and again.

In London I chased a life of instant gratification and selfish ambition, rapt by the trappings of success and the freedoms it afforded from financial stress. It gave me a sense of worth, of purpose – or so I thought – and in the process spawned countless beautiful relationships that I'd systematically tear apart, rinse and repeat.

I conveniently wrote them off to experience: they would help me to grow, shape me into an even bigger rock star. But through the haze of morning light, I always knew it wasn't me. That the kind, generous and humble guy on the other side of the mirror was who I deeply yearned to be, all of the time.

Of course, it was all a necessary part of my journey, simple cause and effect, but what I lacked then was patience. I was screaming out to be heard without any sound, just like in my nightmares. I wasn't representing who I was. The image that stared back at me each morning still wasn't the real me.

There is only so much of living an inauthentic life that one can take and if we don't own up to it, the destructive behaviours will eventually catch up with us, just as they did with Victoria. An undercurrent of discontent had run through my life for far too long; what I needed was a circuit-breaker. And it came in the form of the ladies of the 10 Baht Bar.

At first it represented outward change, to somehow raise awareness in support of their cause, but I'd soon learn that to do that I first needed to step through the mirror. We all need our Kanchanaburi moment and when it comes, we need to recognise it and act on it. Because if we don't, we are not being true to ourselves, to our life's calling, to our "hero's journey" as Victoria would say.

At 49-years-old, my lesson in trust has been a long time coming and I've learned that stepping through the mirror isn't easy. Confronting our true selves is undoubtedly the most challenging thing any of us can do. Part of us still wants to be that bad guy, still identify with him or what he represents. We fear how much we'll change when we reach the other side, because when we do there's no going back.

But what we don't realise is that the other side is paradise. When we do meet our true selves, we don't ever want to go back, because we've finally found our way home.

My red carpet has been riddled with detours and denials. Instead of going outward it took me inward. It taught me to find the connection I'd been missing within myself and helped me find a simple and beautiful alignment with the words in *An Anglican Prayer Book*, it was like cracking the Enigma code.

In his masterful guide to spiritual enlightenment, *The Power of Now*, Eckhart Tolle writes "Enlightenment is a state of wholeness, of being 'at one' and therefore at peace. At one with life in its manifested aspect, the world, as well as with your deepest self and life unmanifested – at one with the Being."[1] The book had been given to me by a girlfriend, but I couldn't make sense of it so put it down. It was only years later that it found me again and now lives by my bedside.

In hindsight, I could never have had the calling when my father did, it found me when I was ready. And now I, too, can take respite in knowing that God has guided me at every turn, bestowed in me the lessons I needed to learn and the wisdom to find my way. Like Charl, Victoria and Jude before me, at the end lies complete surrender, knowing that it's all part of God's plan.

Like any child, we learn not from what we are taught but from what we experience for ourselves. It was only in this way and on my own terms that I could come to understand the fundamental tenets of the Christian faith and finally understand my father, the man of God.

Our personal epiphany

It's a few days after Trinity Sunday and another sermon arrives. This time Dad is preaching about the unbounded nature of the universe. How we have all struggled at times to comprehend the enormity of creation, the vastness of what we can see and the infinite nature of what we can't. He compares it to the Holy Trinity – the Father, Son and Holy Spirit, all as one. How it is complex to understand or define and how, like the universe, God is too great for us to comprehend with mortal minds.

We're back at the early expansion of Christianity and how this Trinitarian theology was misinterpreted by many as heresy. How statements of belief, or creeds, were created to clarify essential points of Christian doctrine, to protect the church and its followers. The Catholic Church, enveloping Anglicanism, worships one God in trinity and trinity in unity. 'I believe and trust in one God, father, son and Holy Spirit,' ring the words of the Apostles Creed. God the creator, God the saviour and God the Holy Spirit. God and man one and the same, omnipotent and ever present.

The epiphany I had in the upstairs study of my Manly townhouse, the feeling of infinite connectedness with all existence, forged not only an intellectual alignment with my father's views but also an experienced connection with God. That is something no-one can ever question or dispute. It has been a feeling all-too-familiar to my father and I need envy him no more.

To have found the answers I've spent my adult life looking for has been nothing short of exhilarating. To finally know in my heart what my father stands for, how he could dedicate his life to serving God and live with the sacrifices he made – that is surely my greatest achievement.

Now, the love I have for the man I grew up to respect and adore is complete. With God, in God and through God. The father and the son, bound by the power of the Holy Spirit.

We don't have to be saints to get the tap on the shoulder and any one of us can have our own personal epiphany. As Oscar Wilde said, "Every saint has a past and every sinner has a future." But how can we label ourselves authentic while we're still flailing around in the dark? When it comes to facing ourselves, there is nowhere to hide. The beautiful thing is, it's never too late.

15

The power of one

Of all the ornate churches and cathedrals I've visited on my travels, the Sistine Chapel is my favourite. Michelangelo's *Creation of Adam* spanning the arched roof is quite something to behold. It left me in awe of such masters of their craft and it is right that we do all that we can to preserve these works for generations to come.

But it means it is this portrayal as an external being, residing in some heavenly realm that will forever influence how people perceive God. It's how we find God in the scriptures, after all, shining down on us from above. When we pray, we pray to the heavens, holding our hands up high in praise. And when Jesus reunited with his father, he ascended into heaven.

Yet it is this anachronistic representation of God that puts so many people off the notion of religion entirely. Even those that sense there may be some kind of higher power simply can't relate to it.

Of course, there are some who take the Bible at its literal word. But stories such as Adam and Eve and Noah's Ark are just that. They were stories intended to explain phenomena long before the concept of science. The story of Adam and Eve long predates Darwin's theory of evolution. Try explaining the concept of a rainbow before understanding light refraction!

But the scriptures also refer extensively to God being within us and it wasn't until I went on my own inward journey that I could understand the true meaning of the words. In John 14:20 Jesus says, 'In that day you will know that I am in my Father and you in me and I in you.' And Paul writes, 'Do you not know that you are a temple of God and that the Spirit of God dwells in you?' to the Corinthians in 3:16. While in Luke's gospel, 17:20 Jesus says, 'For indeed, the kingdom of God is within you.' These are just a handful of examples.

Many other religious and spiritual practices conceptualise God as not human at all, but rather as an entity that is beyond all form – a power mightier than any mortal, not born of the flesh and unable to be seen. And the more I have become exposed to Buddhist and Hindu teachings, extolling alike the virtues of inward salvation, the more I have come to realise their alignment with Christianity.

Finding stillness is at the very heart of Buddhism. 'Peace comes from within, do not seek it without,' Buddha said. He talked of the mind as being just another one of the senses and that by observing the thinking mind, by being present (or "being", as Eckhart Tolle puts it), we can break free from enslavement by our minds.

Hindus pursue knowledge and understanding of truth. They believe in Brahman as the one true God, formless, limitless, all-inclusive and eternal, encompassing everything in the universe. Moksha, or the soul's release from the cycle of death and rebirth, occurs when the soul unites with Brahman by realising its true nature, or unconditional surrender to God. Their sacred texts, the Upanishads refer to our reincarnation with nature in that we merge into the universal soul of the cosmos which they call atman, the Sanskrit word for 'inner self'.

In the Bhagavad Gita, widely acknowledged as the holiest of the Hindu Upanishads, Krishna (God) says to Arjuna (the self) in 4:11 "The whole purpose of every experience, every activity, every faculty, is to turn the human being inward and lead each of us back to our divine source."

The more I learn, the more I realise that my epiphany had merely opened the door to a truth that has been gifted to us since the very first scriptures were made known to man. It's what our forebears recorded because it was singularly the most important legacy they felt compelled to share. The world's best kept secret has been hidden in plain sight for thousands of years. But, like a stereogram, we could only really see it once we knew it was there.

Maharishi Mahesh Yogi equated the state of transcendence during meditation to being one with God, omnipresent, unbounded and infinite. He was always very clear that Transcendental Meditation is not in itself a religion but a technique for finding greater fulfilment through one's chosen beliefs.

He said 'So this [meditation] is useful to man to develop his individuality and then the fully developed man will find his God through his religion. Christians will realise God through Christianity and Muslims will realise God through Islam. But they will become fully developed Christians and fully developed Muslims and fully developed Hindus. So this we say is a technique and not a religion.' He likened all religions to branches of a mango tree, with meditation at the base of the tree, nourishing its roots.

Undoubtedly, the notion that we are all unified in our connection with the same God is jarring for many fixated with their own label and I can appreciate why. For those of us growing up in religious environments, we are by default attached to the dogma we know. It gets ingrained in our belief system to such an extent that we fear to question it. But how can we be so closed minded? God is far too real and powerful to be in the lives of just a chosen few.

Ironically, nowhere is this fixation more brazenly on display than in the Old City itself. Visiting Jerusalem in my early thirties, I felt it my duty to follow the path Jesus walked bearing his cross, to pay homage to the place where he died set inside the Church of the Holy Sepulchre. At the end of the long walk through narrow cobbled streets, dutifully observing each Station of the Cross, I joined a long line to kneel down and kiss the sacred spot, then observed a moment of silence at the site of the tomb where he rose from the dead. As lame as it seemed, it was a powerful experience.

But what struck me the most about that visit was that just a few hundred metres away stands the Wailing Wall, the holiest site of the Jewish faith. And if someone were to climb that wall, ignoring the audacious nature of such an act, they would stumble upon one of the holiest sites of the Muslim faith, the beautifully ornate al-Aqsa Mosque. It stands resplendent with its gold dome inside an approximately 14-hectare compound referred to by Muslims as al-Haram al-Sharif, or the Noble Sanctuary.

The Dome of the Rock is a seventh-century structure believed to be where the Prophet Muhammad ascended to heaven, while Jews believe the compound to be the site where the Biblical temples once stood, deemed too holy to even tread upon.

What is equally striking is the disdain between Christians, Armenians, Jews and Muslims as they pass each other down the Old City's narrow alleyways, each unwavering in their sacrosanct beliefs. The way they openly cast aspersions on one another, so obsessed with their need to be right that they are blind to the blatant, manifest truth. It's poetic in its absurdity, yet over the course of history it has caused more bloodshed than any other idealistic pursuit.

The traditions of the church, meanwhile, have long been eclipsed by the demands of modern society and it's hard to see how stuffy religious dogmas will return to fashion. 'Church just isn't cool,' a Gen-Y colleague told me. Even my parents have accepted that many of the ideals of the church were borne of a different era and that it needs to adapt to more liberal ways to appeal to a mass audience.

It's exactly why finding alignment between the scriptures and the ancient spiritual practices of meditation and breathwork, revived and re-badged in the modern-day era, is so exhilarating. They are rapidly becoming mainstream and changing people's lives in a fundamental way. They are forging new communities every day and just like the lay ministry movement of the church, in time the ripple effect will change society as we know it.

Breathing a new reality

The five-day silent Vipassana retreat I attended in 2021 was set in the Southern Highland bushland of New South Wales.

The programme involved several group meditations a day of up to an hour each, interspersed with walking meditations, yoga and dharma talks. It was an experience of total serenity and immersion with my surroundings, while many of the mindfulness teachings from our highly enlightened guides stuck with me because of their profound simplicity.

The first was an adaptation of 13th century Persian theologian, Rumi – "Stillness is the language of God, everything else is just bad translation." Another was "You cannot get to God through the mind, God is what is beyond the mind." It reminded me of one of the many inspiring conversations I'd had with Jude as he shared the fruits of his contemplation, quoting renowned mathematical physicist Dyson Freeman when he said, "God is what mind becomes when it has passed beyond the scale of our comprehension."

But it was Psalm 46 from the Holy Bible that had the most profound impact – "Be still and know that I am God." These were words I had recited blindly a thousand times, yet it was only hearing them in that setting, on a Buddhist retreat, that I could truly understand them. It was a watershed moment.

But as elated as I was to have discovered the meaning of these texts, I couldn't help but feel a little ashamed of having been blind to them for so long. And as has been the case so often, it was Jude's wise words that I turned to for comfort. We had just finished dinner that evening at Circular Quay and I was expressing my frustration at not having discovered these truths sooner. This beautiful Nigerian man with his blindingly white smile stopped me and said, 'Matthew, you are exactly where you are supposed to be, at exactly the time you are supposed to be here.' Then, like Jude often does, he stayed silent so I could fully comprehend his words. Nowadays, it is knowing that my journey cannot be rushed and being present to the joys of every day that give me peace and lend me patience.

What I have also come to realise is that however people think of God and whether or not they consider the God portrayed in these different religious and spiritual practices to be one and the same, is not for me or anyone else to pass judgement. Personal beliefs are exactly that – personal. Even within my own family we are four siblings raised with the same set of influences, yet we perceive and experience God in very different ways.

What's important is that we find the best belief structures and channels that allow us to get closer to God. Much like my Vipassana retreat, as a Diocesan priest Dad attended silent retreats every year to revitalise spiritually, mentally and physically. What I get from my meditation practice he gets from prayer and silent contemplation. And it was my sister Sarah who first introduced me to breathwork as a channel for connecting with God after her own epiphany.

Like the rest of us, Sarah had no direct experience of God growing up, but she always felt the presence of three angels walking by her side. She sensed them regularly and is the first to acknowledge she couldn't have coped without God and her angels seeing her through her darkest days. It was on many of those days that she would pray for God to take her away so she could be with them.

It was a particularly stressful time in her life when she turned to deep breathing therapy. Raising a young family, managing an all-consuming job and having to move out of their family home was more than she could take. It was a coping mechanism and she'd tried everything else.

Through over-oxygenating the blood in a controlled manner, deep breathing therapy facilitates a rapid transcendence of the mind to help strip away one's vulnerability and surface emotional stresses in need of healing.

It was during a deep breathing workshop that Sarah encountered God for the first time. She was overcome by a sense of immense bliss, in a place where time and space had no meaning. And once she had settled into her altered state, the messages came through loud and clear. 'Stop wanting to die,' said a voice. 'This life I have given you is a blessing. The next step is already waiting for you, you just need to walk into it. There is no reason to be afraid, just trust.'

It was an experience so profound she wanted to stay forever, but on the outside, staccato breathing and unchecked tears caused her instructors to intervene. She heard herself being called back, as if from some distant land, but not before another download. 'You don't have to die to be with me,' the voice said. 'You can be with me exactly where you are.'

Landing back in the room she felt a lightness as if a tremendous weight had been lifted from her body now unencumbered by doubt. A deep sense of comfort flooded her, and for the first time in her life she knew she was exactly where she needed to be, at exactly the time she needed to be there. Jude's very words to me.

Nowadays I practise breathwork regularly, usually on a Sunday morning on Dee Why beach along with a burgeoning community of kindred spirits, followed by plunging into an ice bath. It's a channel through which I can forge an even deeper connection with God, like turbo-charging my meditation practice; it was attending a Wim Hof retreat that I discovered the power of the mind in overcoming the most adverse physical adversities. Through breathing and the power of thought I spent five minutes in an outdoor ice bath in the middle of winter without feeling a thing, in fact, I'd convinced myself I wouldn't – much like Tony Robbins has people walk across fiery coals unscathed.

Like most people I was a natural sceptic at first, but there is something quite humbling about proving to yourself that these things are possible. It is in this way I now believe unequivocally that I can achieve anything as long as I do the work. It has thrown all I know about perceived reality on its head and I now regularly manifest my future through this power of positive intention. We all have exactly the same power … and how liberating would it be to understand that all we need to achieve anything we want is to create the reality in our hearts and minds?

Manifesting a peaceful reality

It is equally empowering to consider that whatever religion we choose to observe, we are part of something much bigger, something that transcends the confines of any particular dogma. Those of us who choose to shun religion, too, or who were never introduced to it – the atheists, naysayers and sceptics – for the most part, they conduct their lives on the same fundamental principles that define all religions and spiritual practices. They seek and represent love in everything they do, because love is what defines our happiness.

What I have come to realise through my experience of God is that God is love. The central source of energy that connects and drives all of us and our infinite environment is the most powerful unifying love, more real than anything we can perceive in the flesh. When I transcend through meditation or breathwork, the very essence of how I feel when I have that connection with God is one of blissful contentment. The more I immerse myself in it, the more I feel a deep-rooted love towards all life that has permanence, like being part of one unified heartbeat.

My spiritual journey has gifted this emphatic realisation. It unifies the physical and non-physical, it is omnipotent and ever present, both within and all around us. The more I immerse myself in communities of like-minded people, whether it's sunrise meditations in Manly or breathwork on Dee Why beach, I see the same realisations in more and more people. We are all drawn to one another, we feel this innate connection to one another that is palpable. How beautiful is it to consider, then, that we are all united in our pursuit of this same love and have been for as long as we have recorded our existence?

Historian Yuval Noah Harari considers religion to be humankind's greatest invention in the name of progress,[2] a way to galvanise the masses in the name of common belief systems for political gain. But while historical references to support this theory may abound, beliefs that have withstood millennia of generational change cannot be fabricated or baseless. This is an undeniable truth underpinning every sect, clan and creed.

Irrespective of how any of us perceive God, what underlies our individual belief systems is faith. Faith, by its very nature, is something we cannot see, taste or touch. It is the same feeling we all share in our hearts. And in each 'wrapper' is the same four-letter word. Again it is Jude's words I am reminded of when we said our goodbyes: 'We are all seeking a closeness to God. And the Glory of God is man fully alive.'

Is it not inconceivable then, to consider a world at peace with itself? To consider Maharishi's dream becoming a reality? And is it not incumbent on all of us, then, who are the keepers of this truth, to help those who are still blind to it to open their eyes?

It is those of us who are prepared to stand up for the truth out of principle that I have come to respect most in my adult life. People like Julian Assange and Edward Snowden knowingly sacrificed their lives because they felt a sense of responsibility, above all else, to share with the world truths that would allow us all to make better choices.

In a rare podcast interview from his Moscow hideout, Edward Snowden told Tim Ferriss: 'You are never further than one decision away from making a difference. It doesn't matter if it's a big or a small difference. Because you don't have to save the world by yourself. In fact you can't. All you have to do is lay down one brick ... so that other people can lay their brick on top of yours, or beside it. And together, step by step, day by day, year by year we build the foundation of something much better. That is the power of civilisation. That is the power that shapes the future.'

I believe that there has never been a more pressing time in our existence as an intelligent species to begin laying down our individual bricks. We have never been more advanced as a society, yet we have never suffered more from stress and mental fatigue, from more anger and violence. We demand so much of ourselves, juggling all kinds of responsibilities and desires, all in the pursuit of contentment that never comes. Whatever goals societal dictates would have us reach, there's another one just down the road.

All the while our euphoria of progress brings new and hidden dangers. Children are born into the toxic world of social media. As if the social pressures we actually get to face are not enough, now they need to learn to face the faceless, like shadow-boxing ghosts. Ghosts that will haunt them far more than the ones we knew.

How is it that in this age of perpetual advancement, suicide rates in the world's most developed nations are nearly 50 per cent higher than in its poorest?[3] There is something so fundamentally wrong with this equation. How can being born into the life of privilege that so many crave, be a greater cause of unhappiness? Yet attempting to persuade the 'have-nots' that they are better off may be both unfathomable and reckless.

The stark reality is that most of us cannot fundamentally change the way we live our lives. We keep tinkering around the edges and adjusting the settings, but it's the same track playing over and over. We do what we know because that's how we're programmed, what modern society has determined we need to aspire to.

How many of us work slavishly for the sole pursuit of our ambition, only to find we've sacrificed the things that matter, such as friendships and spending time with loved ones? How many of us wake up each morning feeling alone and disconnected, or not alone and disconnected, yet continue to repeat the same patterns?

We drift along in our chosen pursuits dogged by a sense that we are unfulfilled, that there is something fundamentally missing. We can't name it or place it, but nothing makes it disappear for long. We do all that we can to distract ourselves from it, or suppress it with alcohol, drugs and shiny new things.

But no matter how fast we run, it's always there when we stop. Because it's not a natural way for us to be.

In *The Four Agreements: a Practical Guide to Personal Freedom*, Mexican author Don Miguel Ruiz talks about self-limiting beliefs and how they rob us of a joyful life. How we are born and raised into a set of agreements with the world and people around us that dictate the course of our lives, creating an existence based on these past patterns that is entirely unnatural.

It resonates so much with me because of its underlying premise – that we are all connected to one another and the world around us, by love. It is fundamentally based on ancient Toltec teachings, the Toltec civilisation ruling a state in Tula, Hidalgo in Mexico through the first millennium. They were considered by the Aztecs to be their intellectual and cultural predecessors.[4]

Don Miguel Ruiz sets out a roadmap for living in a new perception of reality, a self-created world where we don't need to justify our existence. Where we are free to be who we really are, free of conflict with ourselves and others, free of the fear of being judged by others and of the need to be right. Where we have mutual respect for our fellow man, where we don't fear rejection or feel the need to be accepted, where we are not afraid to love or be loved, or to lose anything, even our own lives. Where we love ourselves completely and live with inner peace. The Toltecs called it a new dream. They lived blissfully in this dream for hundreds of years.

Of course, this sounds utterly utopian, but it's the same dream that Buddhists, Christians and Muslims have espoused since their inception. It's just called nirvana, heaven or jannah.

And living in this dream doesn't require us to become martyrs. It is achievable now. One incremental step at a time.

By looking inward, we can find the tools not only to manage the demands of modern life, but also to better connect with one another and the planet on which we depend. Of course, we don't get to achieve all of the ideals Miguel describes straight away, it's a process. But slowly, day by day, month by month, year by year we can turn the dream into a new reality. One brick at a time.

The sad thing is that we have advanced too quickly as a global society and we've been so obsessed with progress and change that we have lost touch with our roots. It has taken the modern revival of an ancient practice for me to find the means to cope and in doing so, discover the real beauty of the life I was born into.

The Vedic, Buddhist, Aboriginal, Hindu, North American Indian and Toltec teachings are among countless others that refer to the sacred bond between man and nature.

Our forebears' daily challenges may have been entirely different to ours, but their daily practices were based on the same principles of living harmonious and joyful lives and of living sustainably off the land. They both understood and felt a deep connection with each other and our planet, as well as what is beyond our comprehension.

The beautiful thing is that we have been re-gifted these tools to achieve an elevation of human consciousness as a collective, to find inner happiness and thereby raise our planetary vibration. I believe that it is in this way that we can and must solve our most pressing existential issues – fear, anxiety, stress, conflict, environmental devastation, disconnection and lack of purpose.

Understanding that each one of us can bring about this essential change should not be the privilege of the few. We depend and thrive on human connection. Now is the time to embrace and elevate this human connection.

How often do we think 'what difference can I make in this world, I am just one person'? But that is entirely the point. Every person on this planet has the opportunity to help elevate human consciousness. Irrespective of race, creed, religion or social standing, we all have the same ability to bring about positive change, for ourselves and for all of humanity. To me, knowing that is undoubtedly the most beautiful part of being alive.

That is what excites me every day.

Our time is now. Mother Nature is calling on us, one at a time. On the other side of the mirror is our true self, waiting patiently. And it is only when we choose to listen that our awakening can begin.

16
The science of flow

The beautiful thing about change is that it's never too late. By breaking from the past and living in the present, we can fundamentally re-shape our future, irrespective of life's circumstances. This is how we start our journey towards a life of flow, the life described by Don Miguel Ruiz.

When we detach from the pre-determined outcomes we've come to accept and open ourselves to our natural course, things begin to happen that we never imagined possible. We get to live a life in which we realise our full potential, one of consummate ease and synchronicity.

'When you're in flow, everything seems close to effortless,' Victoria said. 'Whether it's chance meetings, déjà vu or just picking up on signs, patterns and moments that would otherwise seem like good luck, you're attracting what's meant for you in your higher destiny.'

All we need to do is to be awakened to these signs, like when I was doing my advanced TM technique and Vedic expert, Mr Jenna, asked if I had noticed anything different in my life. Now that I know, I appreciate this ever-increasing life of flow every day. Whether it's arriving at a full car park just as someone's pulling out, a stranger on the bus recommending an inspiring book or an old colleague calling just as I'm thinking about my next hire, it makes me smile every time.

It's Abraham Hicks' path of least resistance, the art of letting things happen naturally. It's listening to our inner voice and the more connected we are to the unified field of energy, the more we are tuned in to the messages that are intended for us. They become louder and clearer and we become more alive to the subtleties of our awareness. The more we realise what is happening, the more willing we are to trust that it's real.

As spiritual beings this concept is a lot easier to digest, but for those that are more scientifically-minded it is entirely more challenging, even bordering on far-fetched. I get tested on it at an intellectual level by friends and acquaintances alike, many of whom I greatly respect. They aren't religious and most haven't had spiritual experiences of their own, so their worlds are naturally more defined by logic and tangibility. I respect their views immensely and it has spurred me to understanding how these two worlds can coexist.

I didn't have to look very hard because there are countless physicists, neuroscientists and biologists who have studied the causal effect of human intentions – the relationship between the chemicals in our brain that determine our emotions and behaviours and human consciousness. People such as the renowned scientist, lecturer and author Dr Joe Dispenza who I came across through another beautiful example of flow.

I was just beginning to contemplate these ideas when I attended a yoga class at my Balgowlah studio. One of the many insightful instructors there talked about Joe Dispenza's work and how he describes the alignment between our bodies and minds and how each of our body's chakras has its own energetic field that we can stimulate through practices like yoga and meditation. When I asked about it after the class her eyes lit up and she recommended his latest book, *Becoming Supernatural*, which I have found to be one of the most credible studies in bridging the scientific and mystical worlds.

Dr Dispenza explains in very simplistic terms how, like everything around us, we are all made up of matter, the fundamental composition of which is energy and how all of this energy is connected, functioning as one unified field of consciousness.

The average adult male has around 36 trillion cells in their body and the average adult female around 28 trillion cells[5], while the number of atoms in each of these human cells is estimated to be approximately 100 trillion[6]. Remarkably, 99.9999999% of the space inside each of these atoms is made up of energy.

Quantum physics or quantum mechanics is the description of the smallest things in existence – molecules and atoms and what they are made of, namely protons, neutrons and electrons, called subatomic particles. It explains how they interact with one another to constitute the fundamental laws of existence.

Each nucleus of an atom is made up of protons and neutrons which constitute 99.9% of its mass, while surrounding the nucleus is a cloud of electrons, each of which occupies its own unique energy level. This means when an atom comes into the vicinity of another atom or group of atoms, their wave functions can overlap, allowing them to bind together into molecules, ions, and salts with their own unique shapes and configurations.[7]

To put into context the space between the nucleus and these orbiting electrons, if the nucleus were the size of a peanut, the atom would be about the size of a baseball stadium. Put another way, if we lost all the dead space inside our atoms, we would each be able to fit into a particle of lead dust and the entire human race would fit into the volume of a sugar cube.[8]

So, in essence, everything we know is made up of space – our entire reality, including space itself, is full of this sea of energy. Meanwhile, quantum physics proves that these particles, or electromagnetic oscillations can be connected despite being billions of light years apart, known as quantum entanglement.[9] This blew Einstein's theory of relativity out of the water, Einstein himself admitting that 'physical objects are not in space, but these objects are spatially extended. In this way the concept of empty space loses its meaning.'[10]

Dr Dispenza has dedicated his life to studying how we can influence this field of energy to shape our futures and even self-heal. He argues that as humans we have the power to change the course of our realities through practices such as meditation. How we can achieve things we never thought possible, like healing ourselves of physical and mental illness, dealing with trauma and forging more meaningful relationships.

After thirty years of training in neurology, neuroscience and cellular biology, Dr Dispenza combines the fields of neuroscience, epigenetics and quantum physics to explore things like spontaneous remissions. He and his team have helped countless people evolve their consciousness so they can heal themselves even of terminal diseases and ultimately live more functional and happy lives.

By conducting brain scans on thousands of students who reported very real, mystical and transcendental subjective experiences during meditation, they have captured these experiences objectively. The tests measured not only functioning brain patterns but also heart rate variability and the corresponding magnetic field around these students as they transmitted information through their enhanced vibrational frequency.[11]

He explains how our body's cells communicate with one another not only via chemical interactions, but also through fields of coherent energy or light, causing the environment around them to give instructions to other cells within their functional system. And how the frequencies of groups sitting in different locations can synchronise through these invisible fields of light, again validated through a series of experiments.

Dr Dispenza and his team brought thousands of meditators together from different locations around the world to demonstrate that as a collective the impact can be entirely more powerful, measuring the changes in energy levels as the number of participants grew.[12]

As I was reading his work it took me back to the epiphany I had after my TM retreat in the Narrabeen bushland. I'd felt robbed because most of the programme involved us repeating sequences of Ayurveda yoga, pranayama and meditation in our rooms, which is called 'rounding'. But what I realised afterwards was that the physical walls were no hindrance to the elevated vibrational frequency each of us experienced, which for me would prove to be most profound.

I have since discovered that there are several peer reviewed articles which have shown how levels of violence, crime and even traffic accidents have been reduced during group meditations, corresponding to periods of sustained economic growth.

For example, between 2007 and 2010 a Transcendental Meditation study was conducted at the Maharishi University of Management in Fairfield, Iowa including 1 725 participants meditating twice a day for 20 minutes. It reported a more than 28% reduction in the murder rate during this period compared to the prior four years in 206 large US urban areas, equating to more than 4 000 lives saved.

Published in the *Journal of Health and Environmental Research*, co-author Dr Michael Dillbeck noted, "This study and 17 other peer-reviewed studies suggest that one's individual consciousness is directly connected to an underlying, universal field of consciousness and that by collectively enlivening that universal field through the Transcendental Meditation technique, such a group can have a positive effect on the quality of life in society."[13]

The co-authors calculated that the probability of this simply being due to chance was 1 in 10 million. They also eliminated the possibility of any causal factors such as unemployment, national economic conditions, changes in incarceration rates, police technology, urban demographics or even reporting standards which could have accounted for the decline. What they found was that during that period, these 206 large urban areas in fact experienced higher poverty rates, lower educational levels, higher unemployment, greater social instability and other predictors of higher rates of violent crime than the rest of the US.

A Reuters article cites the dramatic and unexpected reduction in crime rates in 2009 despite expectations from police chiefs across major US cities that levels of violent crime would continue to escalate. It reads, "Year-end statistics from the largest US cities defy the predictions of many police commanders who braced for a crime wave they expected to be unleashed by the recession, rising home foreclosures and social despair ... last year turned out to be the safest on record in New York City, with the murder rate in the nation's biggest metropolis plunging to its lowest level since the city began gathering comparable data in the early 1960s ... Los Angeles, the second-most populous US city, posted its lowest crime rate in about 50 years ... homicides alone in Los Angeles dropped by 18 percent."[14]

According to the study's other co-author, Dr Kenneth L. Cavanaugh, "The basis for the hypothesized effect on society is that consciousness in its pure form, pure consciousness, has a field-like character and is a universal field at the basis of everyone's thought and behavior. When the participants in a group equal to or exceeding the square root of one percent of the entire population are experiencing pure consciousness during group practice of Transcendental Meditation ... the field of pure consciousness is enlivened in the entire population. This will positively influence all others in society, leading to development in the same holistic direction as experienced by individuals practicing the Transcendental Meditation technique."

The explanation is amazingly simple – when we transcend through meditation or breathwork we enter a state of higher consciousness, the unified field, in which we are more aligned with the laws of nature and with everything and everyone around us. By being present in this state we are able to elevate our own vibration as well as the vibration of our environment, countering the negative vibrations brought about by those who act against the laws of nature, either because they are circumstantially deprived or deeply unhappy within themselves.

What I have also come to further appreciate after that yoga session is the power of alignment between our bodies and minds. Dr Dispenza talks about how the brain and energy centres in our bodies, or chakras, interact and stimulate each other through a dynamic flow of information and how they are controlled by our subconscious Autonomic Nervous System (ANS), which drives all automatic functions beyond the brain's conscious awareness.

He notes that each of these chakras has its own glands, hormones, chemistry and energetic frequency and how we can influence these chakras to operate in a more balanced and integrated way by learning to change our brainwaves and entering our subconscious operating system. We do this through meditation and breathwork by shifting our attention from beta brainwaves, which focus on the outer world, to alpha brainwaves which focus on the inner world.

He determines that in this way, through coherent heart and brain connection, we can break the patterns of our habitual thoughts and feelings and change our gene expression, neural transmitters, hormones, proteins and enzymes to create new realities and alter the internal drivers of our external reality.[15] The building blocks of Don Miguel Ruiz's dream world.

Yoga is now part of my weekly exercise routine, which along with a healthy diet has further strengthened my connection with the unified field of consciousness – with God. This connection lies not externally but within the body, so by focusing my attention inwardly during meditation and staying healthy I have been able to permanently enhance this channel of two-way communication.

Victoria advocates that nurturing our physical, spiritual and emotional habits on a daily basis can help create flow – things like nutrition, rest, exercise, meditation, keeping a journal, gratefulness and positive affirmations.

I know now that fulfilling my dream of coming to Australia was a necessary part of my journey. I needed to become healthy again, to reconnect with nature, to begin my inward quest to meet my true self and discover God on my terms. Sunday mornings now no longer see me sitting in wooden pews, but rather on a surfboard at the back of the line-up, watching the sun appear over the horizon and running my hands through the silky waters of the Pacific. My church is around me all the time and every day I become a little more supernatural.

When I do find myself in church on occasions that call for it, the experience is also entirely more joyful. Now that I've fostered my own connection with God, the emptiness I'd felt as a child has been completely displaced.

It was Christmas 2019 when I last visited my family in Cape Town, just before the world changed. Arriving on 24 December from Sydney, jetlag had me pull out of midnight mass with the family. I just wouldn't have made it past the first prayer, so instead I detoured to St Stephen's the next day on the way to my sister's house for Christmas lunch.

I sat alone in the back pew intent on celebrating the Eucharist with Dad's old parishioners, in relative obscurity. Only this time I wasn't there out of a sense of duty, rather because of an innate yearning, one that I'd only come to fully understand as I choked back tears for most of the 70-minute service. Because sitting in the same pews, surrounded by the same faces, I experienced God inside those four walls for the first time.

The organ churned out the same hymns to the same harmony-bereft voices of young and old and we recited the same worn pages of *An Anglican Prayer Book*. Only this time the words made sense to me, as if they'd jumped off the very pages and rearranged themselves. To a thumping heart I heard God speak to me through the words of the Nicene Creed and when I knelt to pray in reverence, it was God that knelt beside me.

If my heart could have burst, it would have flooded the isles of St Stephen's that Christmas morning. And stepping out into the warm summer air I felt an elation the sort of which is rare in our lifetimes, like I had finally healed an open wound. I no longer saw our compulsion to attend church as an act of hollow authority, but rather one of unfettered goodwill. That we, too, might come to know God and invite him into our daily lives as Mum and Dad had. It was always an act of kindness, against which I'd rebelled in my blindness.

Now I look forward to the occasions when they come, each time finding some new meaning in the Anglican doctrine. And while it has lent a long-lost sense of purpose to the drudgery of my youth, the purpose was always there. Simple cause and effect. It's why we should never seek to change the past, or dwell on it for too long.

It has given me renewed appreciation for the power of prayer, too. My daily meditations and prayers now morph into one, part of a continuous connection with God.

I'm back standing in the hall of our Bredasdorp house, watching my parents speak in tongues, lying on my bed as my father lays his hands on me to ease my suffering. Wiping away tears as the packed church at St Aidan's asks God to give the leaders of our broken South Africa compassion.

As with meditation, numerous studies of brain activity during states of deep prayer have shown changes to both the frontal lobe, which controls our concentration and focus, as well as the parietal lobe, indicating a state of transcendence. These studies have even shown permanent changes to the thickness of the frontal lobe in people who pray and meditate regularly.[16]

According to renowned clinical psychologist and author Michelle Roya Rad, "Prayer and meditation can influence our state of mind, which then have an effect on our state of body. It can help with anxiety, sadness, blood pressure, sleep, digestion and breathing. It also can influence thinking. These, over time, can change the brain activity and ultimately the subjective and objective experiences of us in the world."[17]

It's all part of the same beautiful melting pot, especially when we consider that all the great mystics of their era from Lao Tzu and Dogen to Joan of Arc and Thomas Merton had the same unified mantra – that all we need to reach self-realisation and reconnect with our creator, is already within.

Whichever path we choose, we have the power to change the course of our lives in a meaningful way, just through the power of positive thought and intention. We are what we attract and if we choose to emanate positivity, we can't help but attract that same positivity in return.

Maharishi Mahesh Yogi summed it up perfectly when he said "We are creating a unified world of all positivity. This knowledge is a beautiful thing. Far beyond what is perceptible via science and technology."[18]

oOo

There are many in the scientific community that call Dr Dispenza's work 'pseudoscience'. And of course it's not difficult to selectively endorse a few studies to validate one's own theories, it's one of the beautiful attributes of freedom of speech – we all get to pick our own size and flavour. But what these studies demonstrate makes both intuitive and logical sense to me.

Even if the sceptics are right. Even if, after all the experiments, social studies and scientific papers we cannot prove this connection, isn't the fact that we are able to experience it, enough? It's the same question I keep coming back to. Why is it important to justify scientifically what we can feel intuitively? If I can live a life of bliss, why wouldn't I?

The answer is it's more than enough.

We don't need to live in complete poverty, chastity or obedience, but we can model our lives on the lessons that these disciplines teach us, just as Jude has. We can achieve this based on managing the mind, body and emotions to reach the summit of our spiritual selves and thereby break free from the ties of our past.

I often reflect on the extent to which my faith has been questioned, tested and kicked around. But the beautiful thing is that even if there is no God, even if we're here for no reason whatsoever, just meandering along aimlessly until our time is up, it doesn't matter. The fact that it's given meaning and purpose to so many, nurtured countless relationships, even healed a few assigned to the scrapheap – that alone is enough to pay its dues. There is no reason to justify it via algorithms, science or cognitive psychology.

Cathy Whiteman lived a beautiful life based on a single premise that Jesus loved her. She was flawless in the way she conducted herself, living in God's image. She died one of the happiest people I've known, not a penny to her name. Why would anyone dare deny her that?

In the same way, it is not for us to judge anyone who chooses to live the Toltec dream. This isn't a religion, has no dogma and doesn't require us to make wholesale sacrifices or give up the things that make us happy. That's the reason why we are here, after all. But surely we can find a better balance in which these pleasures are not at the expense of those around us and our beautiful planet.

17
Hey Megan, turn it down

It was the end of a long but happy day. With the numbers three and four still swirling in the evening breeze that drifted into her third-floor apartment, Megan Clancey slumped onto the sofa trying not to spill the last of her bubbles. The cackles of the departing bevy of girlfriends now silenced by the closing lift door, she could finally relish a moment of peace.

The helium balloons twisted and jived over her dining room chair, three before four, four before three. She tried to recall what she'd done on her thirty-fourth birthday, but the Veuve-haze had set in. So with a resigned smile, she closed her eyes to ponder what the year ahead might have in store.

The answer would come faster than she could ever imagine. Not three weeks later, slumped over the steering wheel of her Mazda 3, she was borderline hysterical. The way they'd delivered the news had been so clinical, nonchalant even. Then they peppered it with all that information. Everything swirled round in her head like a thick soup, yet she couldn't help but think that there was a nicer way to deliver a death sentence. And a pamphlet with all the vitals wouldn't have gone amiss. But that's just the way she was programmed, always thinking of how to make things more efficient. It's why she was dubbed 'Council Queen' for the thirteen years she near ran one of Sydney's most salubrious seaside suburbs.

She dived straight into self-deprecation – how could she have gone to the appointment alone, when they'd expressly told her to bring someone? Why was she so stubbornly self-sufficient? And why was asking for help such a struggle? Always the first person that her friends turned to for help, she'd been everyone else's rock. And when she'd needed help, they'd all just shrugged her off 'Oh, you'll be alright, Meegs, you're Wonder Woman.' It's no wonder she'd stopped trying.

Through the flood of tears, she fumbled for her handbag. Despite him being the kindest man she'd ever met, her heart still raced when she called him and his phone starting ringing. She'd only been seeing Pete for three months and he'd already lost his Mum, Dad and brother to cancer.

'Hello darling, how'd it go?' But he didn't need to wait for a response. 'Tell me where you are, I'm coming to get you.'

oOo

Fog filled the passenger seat window to the rhythm of Megan's exhaling; it was about all she could focus on. She loved Pete all the more for trying to comfort her, but silence was what she needed, especially from her own thoughts.

She should have known the minute they checked her in so urgently, but then it was the same medical specialist who'd been so patronising two years before. 'Oh it's probably just haemorrhoids,' she'd said matter-of-factly. As if having the woman's fingers up Megan's backside wasn't demeaning enough. 'Besides, you're too young and there's no history in the family.'

Don't even bother with a colonoscopy, she'd said, better to save the money. So that's what Megan did, getting a second opinion from a pelvic physio instead. 'Just a bit of nerve damage,' this one said while prodding Megan's rectal muscle. It definitely wasn't something she'd get used to. 'Probably too much time on the spin bike.'

How could they not have clocked the golf ball sized tumour nestled just inside? And neither of them cautious enough to look out for other symptoms, or run further tests. So for the next two years Megan watched the blood in her stools get darker and darker, until the pain from sitting became simply unbearable.

Her head jolted against the window. She sat up as they pulled into a familiar-looking driveway, but there was no time for questions. No sooner had the car come to a stop than the passenger door flung open. 'Jesus, Megan.' She felt herself being scooped up. 'Oh my God I'm so, so sorry.' Perhaps it was the sound of her best friend's voice, or just the feeling of being held. Her legs gave in first, then the tears came in earnest.

oOo

'They call it adenocarcinoma,' Megan said after slugging the first of many flutes of champagne that day. It was all Jeeves could do to stop the shaking, bottle at the ready. 'Basically stage 3 bowel cancer.' Pete had made a few calls on his way to Royal North Shore Hospital and the wheels were put in motion. This was to be their home for the next two weeks, surrounded by family and friends, essential during what the doctors call the 'discovery phase'.

But while it was to be the beginning of a long ordeal that would shake Megan's world to the core, it had also been a long time coming. It's why she blamed herself as much as the gaggle of inept specialists and why she believes she talked herself into getting cancer in the first place.

The glandular fever had come seven years earlier, from sharing a water bottle with someone she thought she knew. It would turn into chronically active Epstein-Barr virus or EBV, more commonly known as 'the kissing disease'. It meant she was perpetually exhausted and with her immune system compromised, she was acutely more vulnerable to infections and disease. So she ran blood tests like clockwork. None of them had shown any signs.

For someone that prided herself on getting things done, the constant fatigue was infuriating. It gnawed at the very essence of who she was. The mornings were hardest, trying to scare herself into getting up. 'Get out of bed, you lazy bitch,' she'd shout. And when she could no longer cope, she'd escape to her parents' Adelaide home for recovery. It was there, staring out of the window at the blue South Australia sky that she first knew the only way to heal was to change her mindset.

Despite her best efforts to slow things down, with the stresses of life mounting she'd been working 100-hour weeks. She tried to eat well and self-medicate on vitamins and Chinese herbs, but being boring just wasn't her style. So she'd comforted herself with wine, gorging on her favourite cheeses and processed meats.

Having researched foods associated with cancer, she knew it wasn't good for her, even joking with her butcher every time she stocked up on salami 'You know this is going to give me cancer one day.' But she needed to do things that made her feel good and the patterns kept repeating.

At the same time her career had unravelled before her. Having given her life to the council, they used the amalgamation of three local areas and a changing of the guard as an excuse to toss her out. And when she tried to push for fair compensation, they tied up her redundancy in a fabricated legal battle. So on she toiled, heartbroken, betrayed by the very people she'd called her family.

It wasn't just the news, then, that broke her that day in Royal North Shore carpark, but the realisation that she'd brought it all on herself. And no matter how much Jeeves and her entourage protested, she couldn't hide from her own truth.

oOo

The prognosis wasn't good. The cancer had already gone walkabout, breaking through the bowel tissue wall. A rogue lymph node in her pelvis was a worrying sign and meant a much greater chance of regression.

The tumour had been growing for more than three years and was so big and low down that the surgeons would need to cut out Megan's entire rectum and all its functional ability. No reconstruction would be possible. They'd try and shrink it first to minimise the damage, but best-case scenario was a colostomy bag for life. Worst case – no need for anything.

Stomas came with complications, too – a lifetime of special diets, raw and irritable skin, bowel obstructions, adhesions and reoccurrences. To make matters worse, the initial chemotherapy and radiation would fry her bladder, ovaries, womb and vagina, causing instant menopause. For someone who still clung to the prospect of motherhood, it was a bitter pill to swallow, especially given her natural affinity with children. She was always the one they flocked to, the first to roll around with them telling silly jokes. It would be a burden only to those who knew her well. She'd just faced her greatest fear.

It's times like these that define who we are, existential crises that could never happen to us in our wildest dreams. Yet there we are, staring down the loaded barrel. We can choose one of two ways out – resign to the inevitable and pull the trigger, or try and defy the odds. For Megan there was only ever one option, but it was going to take everything she had, starting with belief. She had nothing to go on except those helpless mornings staring out of the window at their family home, but it was something. And if she was going to fight, it would be with all the sass and spunk that had come to define her 43 years.

oOo

Megan spent the discovery phase doing exactly that. With Jeeves's family laying on everything from dry shoulders to Moët on tap, she threw herself into research. Preventative treatments for chemo and radiotherapy side effects, mostly legal alternative therapies, books, blogs, podcasts on how to deal with cancer. She even plugged herself into bowel cancer chat groups. And under Jeeves's close supervision her entourage sprang into action – drivers, chefs, masseuses and listeners ... with busloads of cheerleaders.

Visitors came and went aplenty, her brother, too, came up from Adelaide. He'd been sent on a mission to bring Megan home, but after two days he'd called their mother to say she was exactly where she needed to be, in a serene ocean setting surrounded by people who loved her. There was nothing she'd get at home that she didn't already have in droves, so he went home empty-handed. And after two weeks of tears, tantrums and pockets of darkness, Megan Clancey decided it was time to put on her big girl's blouse and face the music.

Word travelled fast and with most of Manly already aware that her arse was on the line, there was no point hiding. She wasn't easily embarrassed and if it meant saving her tush, she was all in. So she started an online chat group and recorded on photo and video sharing apps. Documenting the journey would give her a channel to vent, laugh, cry and share, a noticeboard to answer everyone's messages at once. But mostly it allowed her posse to join the fight, #nochanceagainstclancey.

She was going to need them all. Back in the confines of her apartment, reality hit in a big way. Self-employed, being dragged to appointments in every direction and waiting to see busy doctors meant not getting paid and there wasn't much help from the Commonwealth. Petrol, tolls, parking and an assortment of scans – PET, MRI, CT – all in different hospitals, on different days and at different times.

It was all so personal, too. Arriving at Royal North Shore Cancer Centre, she was the next number from the ticket dispenser – first available oncologist, please. Then hauled before a panel to workshop her results. She'd walk out depressed and deflated, not even a lollypop to show for it.

In between the full-time day job and household chores, she had to find time for more research, a new diet, shopping, meal prep, sourcing pills and attending treatments. She was facing mounting costs and an emotional mushroom cloud, all the while fighting fatigue and trying to hold down a relationship.

Despite all the help, she found herself alone in the wilderness. Since telling her parents, she'd yet to hear from her father. He'd gone AWOL, resigned to his deck chair, staring out into the same blue South Australia sky. But it wasn't his own future he pondered, not even his upcoming milestone. The whole family would be gathering, celebrating 80 good years. He'd trade it all in given half a chance of saving his daughter.

oOo

Before starting the descent towards Adelaide airport, Megan stared out over the bank of clouds, startlingly white. Then she slipped on her headphones. It would be a final moment of peace before the chaos, her last hoorah before the treatments started. Despite fearing being a downer, she couldn't miss her father's party. And while living on cucumber sticks and water would be painful, it might just be the last chance to see her cousins, siblings, nephews and nieces. The time was well spent, the goodbyes long and painful. And bawling all the way back to Sydney, she was tossed around like a pinball between denial, ineptitude and the prospect of death.

The tears came in full flow when she reached her Fairlight apartment. Her friend Barbara had let herself in with the spare key and replaced all her makeup and skin care products with natural, organic alternatives, leaving fresh lilies on the dining room table. Slowly she re-opened the message she'd finally received from her father.

'Well, you certainly know how to deliver a knock-out blow … all I can say is that we will fight alongside you. It is going to be a wild ride and pretty rough in places. But I know that you are a fighter and once you decide that something is going to be done and how, you do not let anything get in your way. You will win this battle.'

It was all she'd needed – none of the "I love you's", just that.

A new thought for the day popped up on her public gallery page. 'You will never know how strong you are, until strong is the only choice you have.'

She smiled and closed her laptop. Tomorrow was a brand-new day. It was time to take control.

oOo

'Hi, Clark Kent, it's Wonder Woman.'
'Hello, Megan,' replied Justin her surgeon.
'So, you know this whole 24-hour liquid diet thing before the procedure, I was just wondering whether champagne counted.'
'Is it liquid?'
'Thanks, you're the best.'
'Make sure you drink lots of water, ratio of one to five.'
'Can't wait to save the world with you, Clark Kent.'
'Megan … that's one part champagne and five parts water.'
'Bye, Clark Kent.'

Humour was her secret weapon. And she wasn't afraid to use it. If she was going to believe in herself, she needed her team of specialists to believe in her too and to do absolutely everything in their power to save her. So she had to be noticed.

For every appointment she groomed her long dark hair, she dressed up for the races and splashed on pink lipstick, brighter still against her pale complexion. It pepped her up, too, a distracting reminder of her early brush with modelling all those years before.

Every text message was signed off 'Thank poo' followed by an explosion of emoji's – peach, poo or doughnut. She named her tumour Steve and her arsehole, Alan. It was all about who would be the captain of her shit show and meant she never had to use the words 'tumour' or 'cancer'.

'Barbie Butt' was the name surgeons had given her procedure because it has no hole. She joked about finally having a butt like Barbie and that one less arsehole in the world surely wasn't a bad thing.

Each time she undressed, there was a different tattoo above her backside. 'I love Justin' his assistants found especially amusing, while love hearts where the chemo needle went in got the nurses going every time. It was pure theatre and it worked.

Soon every specialist she'd had trouble getting hold of was calling her. She'd bounce into her appointments with an air of defiance, less 'fuck you, cancer' and more 'I'm not even sick.' She knew the only way to win was to be outwardly positive and make sure they all knew this wasn't Megan Clancey's time to die.

There were dark times and the speed humps kept on coming. She had persistent nightmares, ones so traumatic her body wouldn't let her remember. But the fear was real, rocking back to sleep in Pete's arms for hours. She'd also learned of an old colleague dying of cancer. Until that moment she hadn't even contemplated losing the battle but dispatched the idea just as quickly.

Justin rang and said there was a 6–8 week wait before treatment could start. With Christmas coming there was a ballooning backlog at Royal North Shore. It meant not only a delay but starting just before Christmas day, so she marched in to see her oncologist and asked him to find a solution.

The next day she pulled into the leafy backstreets of St Leonards and entered Mater Catholic Hospital by the back door, past a statue of Mary. It was the same statue that stood outside her high school and the church where her father played the organ. A receptionist named Megan greeted her with a warm smile. Always on the lookout for signs, she'd found her speed. This wasn't a place full of sick people.

oOo

Taking back control was a real turning point. She made sure she wasn't alone for long, hiding her fear through reconnecting with friends. She called on favours one at a time, for emotional support at appointments, taking notes and updating the group chat and driving her to hospital. She cut back her working hours, freeing up mornings for radiation treatments and Fridays for appointments. The specialists would have to work around her – dieticians, gynaecologists, geneticists, counsellors and naturopaths all toeing the line. It meant she had the weekends to freak out and let her hair down, small pockets of normal. Then pull herself together in time for Monday.

The standard of care in Australia is 25 daily sessions combining radiation with chemotherapy. Then 10 weeks for the body to recover and the tumour to shrink, followed by surgery and another six months of intense chemotherapy, the hair-losing kind. There are no other options, no naturopaths or integrated remedies, it's just the way it's always been done, the same as the 1950s.

So she researched every available alternative, making sure they wouldn't interfere with her treatment, then smashed them all. De-wormer for dogs, gin with rainforest herbs, bicarbonate of soda to alkalise the body, daily vitamins and nausea tablets. She bought a filter for drinking pH-balanced water and used only organic skin products to help with the burning. Still, a perpetually raw backside, defecating shards of glass, confronting menstruations and the Big Dry were constant battles. But she pushed through, at the same time as entertaining the troops. It was all part of her show, a build up to the grand finale.

Naturally, it all came at a cost, spending upwards of $1 000 a day on treatments. With little left in the piggy bank, out went the bat signal. Everyone rallied and after the first round of donations her friend Tim started a GoFundMe page raising tens of thousands. Megan was blown away by the gesture, mostly because it also reinforced how many people cared and were just as determined to see her on the other side as she was.

So instead of saving it for after-surgery support she threw the kitchen sink at saving Alan. She used daily infrared saunas and took hyperbaric oxygen, bought vitamins from exotic locations and even THC suppositories from Nimbin. Vices like sugar, coffee, alcohol and dairy were already long consigned to the scrapheap, so she ate only plant-based organic food and drank Kangen water, while sunrises would see her stretched out on a Pilates mat to keep things tight.

She took the first available opening at a Gawler Institute retreat, based on the seven pillars of healing – meditation, power of the mind, effective support, emotional healing, quest for meaning, nutrition and exercise. It wasn't the first time she'd heard that it's those who dedicate their lives to helping others that are most susceptible to cancer and looking around the room, she believed it. Two reiki healers, two nurses, a teacher, a vet and a home carer made up their motley crew. It made perfect sense, always taking in other people's negative energy and seeing their pain, while forgetting to make time for themselves. If she made it out alive, there would be changes.

Inspired by stories of intention-based healing, including by Dr Joe Dispenza and his team, she believed with every fibre in her being that she wouldn't need to roll over on that surgeon's table. She enlisted a partner for daily meditations and used visualisations at every opportunity. When her reiki session was disturbed by building noises next door, with every turning drill she imagined the cancer cells being systematically unscrewed from her body. For half an hour each day she lay in bed picturing little men in white plumbing suits climbing into her backside and chipping away at Steve with hammer and chisel, then flushing out the debris with aqua blue water. She played nature recordings, imagining birds flying in and picking out the worms and a bright white light enveloping her whole body.

With D-Day looming, she called Justin and said surgery had to be pushed back by two weeks. She needed more time and when Royal North Shore got sticky about the date she went to her oncologist and requested a change in surgeon. She said she wasn't feeling the connection but would be prepared to keep him if they shifted the date. Then told them to book in a colonoscopy and PET scan two days prior.

Those were her terms.

oOo

'You know what's going to happen today, Clark Kent?'

'Hello Megan.' It was colonoscopy day, 48 hours before surgery.

'We're going to wake up ... and Steve will be gone.'

Justin sighed. 'Megan, you know that's highly unlikely, don't you.'

'Nope, there's gonna be nooo tumour. You'll see.'

'Okay, Megan. I'll see you soon.'

'Bye, Clark Kent.'

Her post that day read 'Farewell party for Steve at Royal North Shore tonight. Everyone's invited.'

oOo

She was out for a walk in Manly when her phone rang. It was her last chance to stretch her legs before going under the knife. The birds were out in full swing atop the promenade's bank of Norfolk Island Pines.

'Megan, there's no tumour,' said an excited Clark Kent.

She stopped and smiled. 'I told you there'd be no tumour.'

'No, you don't understand. We ran a biopsy and the results just came back. I reviewed them last night with the chemotherapy and radiology team and it's definitive. There are no cancer cells. At all.'

'Yup, I told ya.'

Justin was stumbling over his words as if racing to get them out. 'The MRI and PET scans, there's no evidence of metastasising either. That means there's no need for surgery.

Megan,' there was a pause. 'Alan won.'

And with that they both lost it. Megan felt the tears run as she arched back in laugher. Arms in the air she whipped out a few twirls. Justin was still muttering.

'Okay, okay.' She took a moment to catch her breath. 'What about the chemo?' Having convinced herself there'd be no surgery, it was the six months of intense follow up she'd been dreading most.

'Well, I spoke to your oncologist and to be honest, we don't see the point. Megan, there's no cancer. I just can't believe it.'

She sank to her knees, holding the phone over her heart.

'Thank you, Clark Kent,' she whispered. You've just saved my world.'

'No, Wonder Woman, we saved your world together.'

oOo

Instead of an early night and overdosing on alkaline water, Megan's closest posse gathered in her Fairlight apartment to share a 20-year-old bottle of Penfolds Grange. It was meant for her wedding day or the birth of her first child. This seemed entirely more appropriate.

They prepared everything she'd been starved of for months, slow-cooked beef ragu, chocolate pudding with ice cream and a plate of her favourite cheeses. Then they dialled up some nineties classics and danced around the living room.

A loud rap on the door broke their rhythm. It was her dull neighbours.

'Hey, Megan. The music's pretty loud, do you mind turning it down?'

'It's eight o'clock and we just beat cancer. Go for a walk.'

Take on Me by A-ha burst onto the stereo as the front door closed behind her. She was already half-way back to the living room.

oOo

It's remarkable to reflect on stories like Megan's and the many others, some more inspiring still. She continues hearing them through her 'Bowel Babes' social media group. It's her way of staying connected and giving back. The hours of research and her experiences she passes on to others, perhaps to inspire them to beat their own Steves. But also to make them aware of the things she wished she had known and could have prevented, like having a fused vagina.

And it isn't all happy times, either. Every so often Pete will find her curled up on the couch staring out the window of the Dee Why apartment they share. For every success there are many stark reminders of cancer's stealthy and destructive nature. The cruel thing is, many of the Bowel Babes had no 'evidence of disease' either, only to succumb six months later.

Having struggled to find the right group to start with, Megan had a connection with these people. Many of them had spent a week together at the Gawler Retreat, being vulnerable together and picking one another up when no-one else could, because they just didn't get it. Only now they were leaving behind young children and broken husbands.

Staying connected still requires a lot of energy, but Wonder Woman is up to the task, pink lipstick and all. Sadly, Megan's recovery was so remarkable that some even questioned if she'd made it all up, partly because she'd always looked so good, which is perhaps more of a reflection of their own unhappiness. There will always be those who sow disbelief and seek comfort at the expense of others and they are least likely to notice when God comes knocking. You don't need to scroll far down her posts to find a broken, vulnerable and glamourless Megan Clancey.

She sent a list of the alternate treatments she'd used to her oncologist in the hope they might encourage others to do the same. But it's not in their protocols to acknowledge unverified remedies. 'Whatever you're doing, keep doing it,' was about the closest they got. It's one of the reasons she's taken it on herself.

Those same protocols dictate that her specialists check in on her, make sure she turns up for her six-weekly colonoscopy and PET scan, yet she's the one that has to keep reminding them. Perhaps she'd done too good a job convincing them she wasn't sick.

And perhaps that's for the best. With the onset of COVID-19, the treatments and scans were shelved indefinitely so instead of being on 'watch and wait' status it became more like 'wait and hope.' But with the four powders, three liquids and 22 tablets she now takes morning and night, she's not that worried. Although she does remain eternally grateful – it turns out that had the surgery gone ahead as planned, the chemo would have been put on ice. Her system would have been too compromised.

oOo

These days Megan still has to call about scans and colonoscopies every three months while the research is unceasing and all part of being in control in case of a reoccurrence. Given her remarkable journey, it's easy to forget the Epstein-Barr virus that still lurks in the background, so she takes herself for six-monthly sinus and throat cancer checks, too. It's all she can do to keep the anxiety in check.

There are still constant pains she can't work out and sometimes it's wrapped in darkness. Permanent nerve damage in her right hand is frustrating, one of the few side effects she couldn't catch, which means she's no longer fiercely independent. But she can live with it and now happily invests more time in herself. She's also a lot more selective about who she says yes to when they cry out for help.

Despite still meditating regularly, it's maintaining a strong mindset that remains her biggest struggle. She's the first to admit she's a great sprinter when it's required but sucks at marathons and will have this hanging over her for the rest of her days. But she cherishes each day and lives it to the full, especially when she gets to let her hair down. There's always a bottle of Veuve in the fridge, just no salami.

18
The ego trap

Reading about Dr Joe Dispenza's work is inspiring enough, but seeing it in action first hand is entirely more powerful. How awesome is it to think that we all have the same innate ability to create more wholesome futures, even self-heal from potentially terminal disease? Yes we have to do the work, but we also need to believe, not just fantasise or hope but know without harbouring any doubt. The world would have been a shade more melancholy had Megan chosen not to believe. Now she gets to inspire others and help them overcome their doubts, pink lipstick and all.

One of the traits I find so remarkable in Charl, Victoria and Jude is that of being completely devoid of ego. It's the consequence of reaching the point of complete surrender, of knowing that your life is no longer your own and that you are just a vessel for doing God's work. They got there in their own ways and while I have no doubt that I, too, am doing God's work, shedding the ego remains my greatest hurdle.

For most of us it is surely one of the most difficult things to comprehend, let alone achieve. Our job as individuals is to unravel the filters, constructs and beliefs that keep us away from truth, while our ego's job is to reinforce them. As living creatures we all have an inherent survival instinct to protect ourselves from external physical dangers as well as internal emotional dangers. Our ego plays an important part in this, while our brains are hard wired to remember negative experiences and emotions far more than positive ones.

This makes total sense in a world where we're under constant threat. We're unlikely to eat something poisonous twice because our brain makes a point of remembering the experience. In the context of modern times, having a car accident when turning a particular corner means we're much more likely to approach it with caution the next time.

But it also means that we constantly chastise ourselves for the things we didn't do well enough and are much less inclined to retain the things we did do well, or that give us joy. Neuropsychologist Dr Rick Hanson in his book *Hardwiring Happiness* talks about this negativity bias, how our brain is like Velcro◊ for negative experiences and Teflon⎕ for positive ones.[19] We have a tendency towards resentment, regret and pessimism and a heightened sensitivity to stress and anxiety. And we hold on to our negative emotional memories and grudges because we don't want to relive those moments of hurt and trauma.

It's taken me a long time to own this realisation but since the traumatic separation from Karina in my twenties, I've never allowed myself to be fully vulnerable. Each time I get close to someone my ego takes over, leading me to focus on their flaws rather than my own. The eventual consequence, each time, is inevitable.

But I have also come to understand that throughout my adult life I have been subconsciously chasing a sense of wholeness that I believed I would find in someone else, solely because it was the only way I knew how. As a result, what I looked for in a chosen partner was something they simply could never provide. Despite their amazing attributes, of which there have been many, they were never going to fill the void inside me. I needed to do that by myself and for myself – I couldn't understand that until I learned to find wholeness within.

But despite this ever-growing self-love I still often fall into the ego trap. It feels a pipedream to shed vanity entirely or to stop chasing the same things society would have me value. So I regularly ask myself, can we really be entirely devoid of ego? The answer I get to is the same as it is for most things – be patient and keep doing the work, everything else will take care of itself.

According to Dr Hanson, by consciously focusing more on our positive experiences, both past and present – and how they make us feel – we can actually rewire our neural pathways to live with greater self-compassion, confidence, gratitude and contentment. Meditation, prayer, doing things that make us happy and taking the time to appreciate them, being grateful for beautiful moments in our past – these are all things we can do to vastly improve our quality of life.

So many people are under the illusion that one day they'll wake up and just be enlightened or content. But what they fail to realise is that enlightenment and contentment is what is happening to them every day that they take the time to invest in themselves. It's such a gradual process we hardly even notice it. Just like learning to play the guitar, we don't just decide to pick it up one day and smash out our favourite rock ballad, it's a skill that our body and mind need to learn.

It takes dedication and perseverance. In this world of instant gratification there are many who don't have the patience for it, which is why breathwork has become so popular. To me it's an accelerant to the beautiful place I get to in deep transcendence, after years of practising. But whatever we choose our channel to be, as long as we stick to it, the rewards are immeasurable. Little by little, day by day we feel a bit lighter yet more grounded, we stop caring about the things that used to bother us and we find our relationships to be more wholesome and less conflicted. We discover what it is to be truly happy, bursting at the seams with gratefulness for life's riches that surround us every day. We stop dwelling on our past failures or obsessing about what comes next. Another step closer to the Toltec dream.

The Greeks have many different words for love. From *eros*, the romantic and passionate love, to *philia*, a soulful love we develop through close friendships and *pragma*, a committed and compassionate love of family. They also include *philautia*, a love of self and *agape*, an empathetic, universal love, a love of God, nature and strangers, or those that are less fortunate.

We find ourselves more and more in love in these different ways and when we are, our egos are nowhere to be found. Yes they will creep in and we'll find ourselves challenged by the circumstances of daily life, that's a given. But it's how we deal with these circumstances that changes and how we interact with others in the process. We bring more balance to our lives and with it, greater flow.

The real beauty of it is that our journey is never ending. The more time we spend being present, being in the vortex, being closer to God, the more enlightened we become. By detaching from the stresses of life, by observing them from a place of stillness, over time we are no longer affected by them. We take them in our stride and most importantly, we find ourselves being non-judgemental.

Writing this book has been a cathartic experience. I have learned so much about myself in the process and about what's important to me. I have also asked myself along the way what my own greatest lesson has been. The answer was surprisingly clear and simple.

Forgiveness.

Our ability to forgive is the only way we can truly love ourselves. Whether we like it or not, grudges we hold against people, no matter how trivial, stay stored in our subconscious. Every time we see those people the same biases re-emerge, only each time with less contrition. Learning to forgive them is a good place to start.

But the ultimate forgiveness we need is of ourselves. Forgiveness for all the things we've done or haven't done, all the times we let ourselves down, made excuses or lied. All the times we could have done things differently, said things differently, or not said anything at all. The times we hurt the people we care about, or didn't help when we could have, even strangers.

Victoria couldn't love herself until she forgave her father for what he did. Once she did, she was finally able to forgive herself. The self-blame she carried for all those years, the burden of what ifs. What if she'd behaved differently, what if she'd spoken up sooner, what if she'd just said 'no'. But she didn't, because she couldn't, because she didn't know it then.

Charl couldn't love himself until he forgave his wife for taking away his children and until he forgave the perpetrators who walked onto his neighbour's farm and shot him in cold blood. Only then could he fully open his heart to God and allow himself to forgive the only person he ever blamed. Himself.

Jude couldn't love himself until he had the forgiveness of his parents for walking out of Blackfriars Hall that crisp autumnal morning. Until he forgave himself for not getting on an earlier flight to see his brother Paul one last time. Even seven years in a monastery can't stop you from bearing that.

And my father can never really love himself until he learns to forgive Staggie, the notorious Cape Town ganglord-turned-born-again Christian. Until he forgives himself for the inadequacy of not being able to provide materially for his children, his four successful, wholesome, happy and loving children.

Throughout our lives we experience loss in many forms. What I have come to realise is that it's important to mourn, to reflect and appreciate, so that we can take the learnings intended for us. But we can only do that when we find acceptance and it is only in finding acceptance that we can forgive. This is our ultimate turning point, just as it was for Charl, Victoria and for Jude.

It took me a long time to accept Mike's death. That came only through appreciation for what it has taught me and the direction it has taken me. Now, I can honestly say that I am able to rejoice in it. In part this is also because I understand where it is that he wrote to us from, that place which is more beautiful than we could ever imagine. Paradoxically, I have never held any resentment towards the driver that night, rather just a deep empathy for the turmoil he must have endured. I hope that he has learned to forgive himself.

So many of my fellow South Africans experienced loss at the hands of the State that it is difficult for me to comprehend. Loss of the right to a dignified life, loss of any opportunity to realise their potential, loss of feeling welcome in their own country. Loss of their loved ones through senseless murder and violence. Loss of the freedom of generations then and now. How must it feel to lose your child, then spend your life wondering where they might be buried?

The Truth and Reconciliation Commission was a bold and novel attempt to heal the country's gaping wounds, run not by the judiciary but rather by leaders of the church. By sober jurists whose sole purpose was not justice, as so many advocated for, but rather to give the people of South Africa the chance to find acceptance and in doing so, learn to forgive.

For the many that talked openly of their loss it undoubtedly unearthed a great deal of pain, while for the most part their perpetrators sitting before them showed genuine remorse. But there were some that sat stone-faced and stone-hearted and there were many of the most deserving who were not called to account at all, on both sides. No doubt it wasn't perfect, but it did give those who were stuck in the past, a chance to move on, to learn and to accept. Perhaps to forgive. And in spite of the country's many failings, there remains a wellspring of goodwill in South Africa that is steeped in hope.

Nelson Mandela spent 26 years in prison, 18 of which were in a room two metres by two metres of steel and cold concrete floor. When he walked free, he embraced those who put him there and opened his heart to the nation. Because some time during those long, cold, lonely nights he learned to forgive, both them and himself. My hope is that this legacy will endure for generations to come, so that Charl's wish of a country where everyone is treated fairly and justly might come true.

I take daily comfort in the fact that I can't change the past. I am here, now, exactly where I am supposed to be, because this is my chosen path. I can't learn things any faster or force myself to make better decisions. I make the choices I do for the reasons I do, because it's what feels right. I understand that fear is the greatest inhibitor of my progress and I have learned that it is only in being bold that I can achieve all that I seek to do. It means I will keep making mistakes, but I've long since learned to forgive myself, because I trust myself now that it always comes from a place of good intent. And I believe beyond doubt that anything is possible.

We all have the power to forgive. It's our mightiest weapon. It will disarm any enemy and build bridges capable of crossing any divide. It is how we can forge new pathways to freedom and living joyful lives. All we need to do is open the door and look inside. All the answers are there, they always have been.

19
Heaven on earth

When I was five, my brother Richard and I pleaded with Mum to take us across the road so we could play with our Bredasdorp neighbours. Between our houses ran Long Street, the main road bearing much of the town's corridor traffic, so crossing without supervision was strictly off limits.

With dinner already being prepared, Mum refused. So tiptoeing to the front door, Richard lifted me up to undo the safety latch, then quietly closed the door behind us as we slipped out. Once clear, we bolted through the gate straight onto Long Street.

All I recall in that moment was glancing to my right, only to see the shiny silver grille of a double-decker bus hurtling towards my face. There was no sound, just a slowing of time as the neatly-polished lines came towards me, as if I was staring down into a giant toaster.

Everything came to a standstill.

My senses returned with her shriek as Mum ran down our front steps. Then the sickening smell of burnt rubber. Richard, on my left, looked equally bewildered as the commotion unfolded around us. The uniformed bus driver, chalk-pale, coins in his change belt clinking as he shook, was taken inside and given sugar water to drink. Mum, meanwhile, was an ocean of calm.

We never got to play with the neighbours that day or for weeks after. And it wasn't until much later in life that I realised just how fortunate we are to still be here. Even later still before Mum confessed it was she who needed the sugar water that day, or something much stronger.

It's after moments like these that we fall on our knees in prayer. These experiences can define our faith or test it to breaking point ... like if I'd taken another second or two to reach the latch.

It's those who find themselves on the wrong side of these sliding door moments and who still learn to forgive God that I admire most, like Mike's parents. But that is the very nature of true faith. It transcends human experiences and in time we come to understand that these experiences are themselves transient. They are there for a purpose, all part of our journey.

'Liberation is letting go of the past,' Jude said. 'Nothing lasts long enough for it to be permanent, everything is transient.' It's the vow of poverty at work. He keeps a small pouch in his office with cuttings of Paul's beard so he can be reminded of his brother's scent and momentarily celebrate his life. But then he always moves on.

Jude has in no small way helped shepherd my journey of self-discovery. It was through him that I could align the teachings of the Christian faith with my inward experience. The day he walked out of Blackfriars Hall was the day he found his purpose, because he was brave enough to listen and to trust that it was part of God's plan. Now he shares the fruits of his contemplation with the world. Nothing gives him more joy and we are the richer for it.

It was on the fourth evening of my Vipassana retreat that the full moon hung low over Wilton, New South Wales. It was a crisp but cloudless night, like each of the days before. Its radiance masked much of the canopy of stars, just the Southern Cross glowing on the other side of the night sky like diamonds spilled on velvet. As I stood mesmerised, God's message came through loud and clear. 'Never again will you be lost and always will you have light in your darkness'.

I thought of Charl that cold autumn night, as I do every time I see the full moon now. I saw him taking Liesel and the kids to the top of the *koppie* (hillock) beside their house to watch the moon rise, then sit them down after supper to read from his Bible. This time it's Matthew 5:14: 'When we are turned to face the majesty of Almighty God, when we surrender to Him and seek Him with all our hearts, we reflect His glory.' His message is simple: just like the moon has no light of its own but reflects that of the sun, so it is that we radiate God's light from within.

The words as we sat across the kitchen table drinking our last cup of coffee together will always ring clear in my mind. 'To know the truth, is to know God. And once we know God, we have found our purpose.' I reflect on the long and winding road Charl had to take to find his purpose and how at every turn he overcame hopelessness because he never stopped accepting and trusting. And I wonder how many more full moons will have to pass before I get to pitch a tent on his farm, on some land he knows he'll keep.

In the meantime, Victoria and Liam share her Newport home's sweeping Northern

Beaches vista, providing plenty of inspiration, as does seeing Hello Coach go from strength to strength. Her purpose is to see it heal the hearts of the masses and she works tirelessly to fulfil that every day. She is living out God's plan – not out of ego – but out of trust. In that, she is at peace.

I reflect on the message Sarah received when she first encountered God: 'This life I have given you is a blessing. The next step is already waiting for you, you just need to walk into it. There is no reason to be afraid, just trust.' It's the same message that God has for all of us: Charl, Jude and Victoria found their paths to understanding because they were brave enough to listen. My path to understanding God was in understanding my father and what a joyful one it has been. What is yours?

oOo

I've often thought about my brother and me running onto busy Long Street that day. Along my journey it is the concept of heaven and hell that has occupied so much of my contemplation. What does happen when we take those extra few seconds to undo the latch?

I've watched documentaries and read a few accounts of people's near-death experiences. There is a series of features that seem to preface each of them, a feeling of intense bliss, a sense of lightness, of freedom from burden in a reality beyond time and space. There is also an overwhelming sense of comfort, like finally going home. It's depicted in different ways but always enveloped in pure, white light.

After the experience, many find it hard to reconcile with life. They are unable to reintegrate with a way of living that is fraught with perpetual sadness, disillusionment, fear, anger, hatred and disconnection. They struggle to find happiness and rather find themselves dreaming of returning to that place of unyielding peace. Is it because when we are reunited with God, in returning to source energy, we simply cannot bear to be anywhere else?

The concept of heaven and hell has been much written and speculated about. The depiction of fire and brimstone was an association much exploited by the early church as a way to cajole people into following righteous ways and succumbing to repentance, while harps strum beneath the fingers of angels high above.

For much of my life the most plausible explanation was of reunification with God, as described by those having near death experiences. Hell was simply being exposed to this reunification and then being removed from it, left to roam the ether in remorseful purgatory. It's served as a deterrent, while brushing with God daily has me ever more excited about the day I fully return. The only thing more thrilling than the idea I will grow gradually more joyful over the next 50 years, is knowing that the last breath I take, will be my happiest.

But it was only very recently, as I sought to write the ending to this book that a new perception of heaven and hell became more compelling still. It is a concept once again extolled by Tolle and while it excites me beyond words, his words so ably captured it.

In *The Power of Now*, Eckhart Tolle talks about our consciousness creating the world we inhabit. How it interprets and interacts with the molecular energy dance of the universe.[21]

'If you perceive, on a deep level, separation and the struggle for survival, then you see that belief reflected all around you and your perceptions are governed by fear. You inhabit a world of death and of bodies fighting, killing and devouring each other,' he writes. All that's missing is the flames.

He is referring to the world we create through the egoic mind, one dominated by fear and layers of negativity accumulated in the collective human psyche. And how as we are all connected to each other and the world around us, when the majority of humans become free of egoic delusion, this inner change will affect all of creation and we will begin to inhabit a whole new world.[20]

It is the ultimate shift in planetary consciousness, of finding heaven on earth through raising our collective vibration. It's living the Toltec dream. It's Maharishi's dream of a world at peace with itself.

And as I turn to the scriptures for validation, I find it littered with references. Asked by the Pharisees when the kingdom of God would come, Luke answers in 17:20-21 'The kingdom of God is not coming with signs to be observed, nor will they say, 'Look, here it is!' or 'There!' for behold, the kingdom of God is in the midst of you.'

I do not believe that there will be a second coming in the form of some existential or apocalyptic event. Nor that there will be a judgement of our deeds at the pearly gates. Rather, I believe that in becoming spiritually awakened we can enter the kingdom of heaven right now, right here on earth as echoed in God's words to Sarah 'You don't have to die to be with me. You can be with me exactly where you are.'

We don't have to wait until the end of our days like some grand revelation. The revelation comes to each of us while we are still here.

And now, some 40 years since I started blindly reciting The Lord's Prayer in the pews of All Saints Bredasdorp, I finally understand the words. 'Thy kingdom come, thy will be done, on earth as it is in heaven.'

oOo

We are all from different walks of life yet we stride alongside one another to find the same simple truth. Many people will struggle to let go of the idea that their dogma is the only way. In many cases it's all they have to cling to. It is only when they can identify with that and have the confidence to let go that they can find what they seek.

When we step through the mirror there is no turning back, because there is nothing more powerful, more beautiful or more compelling than the love we have of ourselves. And nothing more that we can ever seek, because we have found our truth.

In John's gospel, 8:32 Jesus said, 'If you continue in my word, you are truly my disciples. Then you will know the truth and the truth will set you free.'

oOo

There is undoubtedly an awakening happening on a global scale and it's growing faster than Facebook can make new friends. We are reviving practices long buried with lost civilisations, forging connections between the world we know and those beyond it that would see us succeed. We are rediscovering that it is only through harnessing our inner power that we can achieve our true purpose as humanity.

What truly inspires me is that there are millions like me who seek this higher purpose. And that many, many of them will act on this revolutionary whim. That is all it takes. Pandora's Box doesn't close for good reason.

What comes next? I have no idea, but the light from Pandora's Box is the purest white. Looking back, it's those parting words of every service that I blindly recited without meaning, in which I now find the most meaning: 'May the peace of God, which passes all understanding, keep your hearts and minds in the knowledge and love of God.'

Like many people perhaps, I feel my life has been spent learning to fly. Now I stand on the clifftop, the sea breeze fills my celestial wings, I take a deep breath and lean forward.

The view from up here is spectacular.

Acknowledgements

A friend who is also a fellow writer said to me recently, "You cannot underestimate the value of a good editor." Never has a truer word been spoken. As I have now come to rely on, but still so deeply appreciate, my introduction to Fiona Brophy was quite serendipitous. And from our very first interaction I knew she was the one.

Through our work together she has not only helped bring this book to life but also given it a shade of her, for which it is all the richer. I now consider her a friend and mentor, too, having learned so much from her own story and amazing craft. My hope is that we get to work together for years to come.

My sincere thanks also to Charl, Victoria, Jude and Megan for being brave enough to allow me to share their stories. Above all it is to Victoria that I owe a deep gratitude for her friendship, guidance and support and to Jude for his example, wisdom and endless grace. Nothing gives me more joy than knowing our lives will always be intertwined.

Finally, to my parents, for showing all four of us children the way, for their boundless love and for the sacrifices they made so willingly so that we might become our best selves. I hope they have found peace in knowing that what they gave us was more than enough.

oOo

I may have written these words, but it has been clear to me from the start that this is God's work. It's why, irrespective of the seemingly endless toil, the self-doubt and the many setbacks it has been such a joyful experience.

The best part is that this is just the beginning. There are many chapters still to be written. I just need to live them first.

Endnotes

1 Tolle, E. (2004). *The Power of Now,* Australia: Hodder.
2 Harari, Y.N. (2011). *Sapiens, A Brief History of Humankind.* London: Vintage.
3 Khazaei, S., Armanmehr, V., Nematollahi, S., Rezaeian, S., Khazaei, S. (2017). *Journal of Epidemiology and Global Health.* Elsevier Ltd.
4 Iverson, SD. (2017). 'The Enduring Toltecs: History and Truth During the Aztec-to-Colonial Transition at Tula, Hidalgo', *Journal of Archaeological Method and Theory.* Springer.
5 Murugesu, J.A (2023). *We know how many cells there are in the human body.* New Scientist, published online 18 September 2023, available at: https://www.newscientist.com/article/2392685-we-now-know-how-many-cells-there-are-in-the-human-body/
6 Helmenstine, A.M. (2019) *How Many Atoms Are There in a Human Cell?.* ThoughtCo, published online 7 October 2019, available at: https://www.thoughtco.com/how-many-atoms-in-human-cell-603882
7 Siegel, E. (2021) *How All Of Physics Exists Inside A Single Atom.* Forbes Media.

8   Mehrotra, S. (2019) *The Cosmic Dance*. Science and Nonduality, published online 16 May 2019, available at: https://scienceandnonduality.com/article/the-cosmic-dance/

9   Wilczek, F. (2016) Entanglement Made Simple. Quanta Magazine, published online 28 April 2016, available at: https://www.quantamagazine.org/entanglement-made-simple-20160428/#

10 Wilczek, F. (2016) Entanglement Made Simple. Quanta Magazine, published online 28 April 2016, available at: https://www.quantamagazine.org/entanglement-made-simple-20160428/#

11 Dr Dispenza, J. (2017). *Becoming Supernatural: How Common People are Doing the Uncommon.* Hay House Inc.

12 Dr Dispenza, J. (2017). *Becoming Supernatural: How Common People are Doing the Uncommon.* Hay House Inc.

13 Cavanaugh, K., Dillbeck, M. (2017*).* 'Field Effects of Consciousness and Reduction in U.S. Urban Murder Rates: Evaluation of a Prospective Quasi-Experiment, *Journal of Health and Environmental Research*, volume 3. Fairfield, Iowa, USA.

14 Gorman, S. (2010) *U.S. crime falls despite prolonged recession*, Reuters, published online 8 January 2010, available at: https://www.reuters.com/article/us-usa-crime-idUSTRE60613K20100107

15 Dr Dispenza, J. (2017). *Becoming Supernatural: How Common People are Doing the Uncommon.* Hay House Inc.

16 Newberg, A. (2016) 'How God Changes Your Brain: An Introduction to Jewish Neurotheology', *CCAR Journal: The Reform Jewish Quarterly*, available online at: https://static1.squarespace.com/static/52402ca4e4b0b7dd2fafe453/t/57166abb22482e87df44b4d9/1461086907907/how-god-changes-your-brain.pdf

17 Rad, M. (2011) The Power of Prayer: Why Does it Work?. Huffington Post, published online 24 October 2011, available at: https://www.huffpost.com/entry/power-of-prayer_b_1015475

18 Mason, P. (1994). *Maharishi Mahesh Yogi, The biography of the man who gave transcendental meditation to the world*, Element Books Limited.

19 Dr Hanson, R. (2015). *Hardwiring Happiness: The Practical Science of Reshaping Your Brain—and Your Life*, Rider-Trade.

20 Tolle, E. (2004). *The Power of Now,* Australia: Hodder.

www.themangotree.me

Matthew's official website

www.ingramcontent.com/pod-product-compliance
Lightning Source LLC
Chambersburg PA
CBHW060553080526
44585CB00013B/549